A LETTER FROM PETER MUNK

Since we started the Munk Debates, my wife, Melanie, and I have been deeply gratified at how quickly they have captured the public's imagination. From the time of our first event in May 2008, we have hosted what I believe are some of the most exciting public policy debates in Canada and internationally. Global in focus, the Munk Debates have tackled a range of issues, such as humanitarian intervention, the effectiveness of foreign aid, the threat of global warming, religion's impact on geopolitics, the rise of China, and the decline of Europe. These compelling topics have served as intellectual and ethical grist for some of the world's most important thinkers and doers, from Henry Kissinger to Tony Blair, Christopher Hitchens to Paul Krugman, Peter Mandelson to Fareed Zakaria.

The issues raised at the Munk Debates have not only fostered public awareness, but they have also helped many of us become more involved and, therefore, less intimidated by the concept of globalization. It is so easy to be inward-looking. It is so easy to be xenophobic. It is so easy to be nationalistic. It is hard to go into the unknown. Globalization, for many people, is an abstract concept at best. The purpose of this debate series is to help people feel more familiar with our fast-changing world and more comfortable participating in the universal dialogue about the issues and events that will shape our collective future.

I don't need to tell you that there are many, many burning issues. Global warming, the plight of extreme poverty, genocide, or our shaky financial order — these are just a few of the critical issues that matter to people. And it seems to me, and to my foundation board members, that the quality of the public dialogue on these critical issues diminishes in direct proportion to the salience and number of issues clamouring for our attention. By trying to highlight the most important issues at crucial moments in the global conversation, these debates not only profile the ideas and opinions of some of the world's brightest thinkers, but they also crystallize public passion and knowledge, helping to tackle some of the challenges confronting humankind.

I have learned in life — and I'm sure many of you will share this view — that challenges bring out the best in us. I hope you'll agree that the participants in these debates challenge not only each other but also each of us to think clearly and logically about important problems facing our world.

Peter Munk
Founder, Aurea Foundation
Toronto, Ontario

DOES STATE SPYING MAKE US SAFER?

HAYDEN AND DERSHOWITZ VS. GREENWALD AND OHANIAN

THE MUNK DEBATE ON MASS SURVEILLANCE

Edited by Rudyard Griffiths

ANANSI

This edition published in 2014 by
House of Anansi Press Inc.
110 Spadina Avenue, Suite 801
Toronto, ON, M5V 2K4
Tel. 416-363-4343
Fax 416-363-1017
www.houseofanansi.com

Distributed in Canada by
HarperCollins Canada Ltd.
1995 Markham Road
Scarborough, ON, M1B 5M8
Toll free tel. 1-800-387-0117

Distributed in the United States by
Publishers Group West
1700 Fourth Street
Berkeley, CA 94710
Toll free tel. 1-800-788-3123

House of Anansi Press is committed to protecting our natural environment.
As part of our efforts, the interior of this book is printed on paper that contains 100%
post-consumer recycled fibres, is acid-free, and is processed chlorine-free.

18 17 16 15 14   1 2 3 4 5

Library and Archives Canada Cataloguing in Publication
Does state spying make us safer? : the Munk Debate on Mass Surveillance / Michael
Hayden, Alan Dershowitz, Glenn Greenwald, Alexis Ohanian.

(Munk debates) Debate held May 2, 2014, in Toronto, Ontario.
Issued in print and electronic formats.
ISBN: 978-1-77089-841-7 (pbk.). ISBN: 978-1-77089-842-4 (html).

1. Intelligence service. 2. National security. 3. Internal security. I. Dershowitz, Alan M.,
panelist II. Greenwald, Glenn, panelist III. Ohanian, Alexis, 1983–, panelist IV. Hayden,
Michael, 1945– panelist V. Series: Munk debates

JF1525.I6D63 2014   327.12   C2014-904720-7
                                               C2014-904721-5

Library of Congress Control Number: 2014911686

Cover design: Alysia Shewchuk
Typesetting: Laura Brady

  Canada Council
for the Arts
Conseil des Arts
du Canada
 ONTARIO ARTS COUNCIL
CONSEIL DES ARTS DE L'ONTARIO

*We acknowledge for their financial support of our publishing program
the Canada Council for the Arts, the Ontario Arts Council, and the Government of Canada
through the Canada Book Fund.*

Printed and bound in Canada

MIX
Paper from
responsible sources
FSC® C004071

ANCIENT FOREST ™
FRIENDLY

CONTENTS

INTRODUCTION BY RUDYARD GRIFFITHS

State surveillance is the controversy of our time, combining fast-changing technology, the ongoing revolution in how we communicate with each other, the power and responsibility of nation-states to defend themselves, and our deep-seated, personal expectations for privacy — it engages a host of the major tenets that make up our modern way of life. This is why it was an obvious choice for the Munk Debates to dedicate one of its semi-annual contests to bringing together the most trenchant and salient commentators on state surveillance today for a no-holds-barred discussion.

The resolution before the three thousand attendees who filled Toronto's Roy Thompson Hall to capacity was as stark as it was significant: "Be it resolved: state surveillance is a legitimate defence of our freedoms." Speaking for the resolution, in his first-ever public debate, was General Michael Hayden. Considered by many to be the chief architect of the sophisticated surveillance programs that evolved in the post-9/11 era, General Hayden led both the National Security Agency (NSA) and the Central Intelligence Agency (CIA) under President George W. Bush. Throughout the debate, he displayed his unparalleled knowledge of the inner workings and larger policy objectives of America's surveillance networks. In this regard, readers will want to pay special attention to his fascinating account of the 9/11 terrorists and how, in his view, a robust regime of state surveillance such as the one America has today could have helped foil such an attack. To quote Michael Hayden from the debate: "Terrorism is a big deal, but we do [mass surveillance] for lots of good, legitimate reasons. . . . if this metadata program — which is about terrorism, because the only reason you can use metadata is to stop terror attacks, no other purpose — had been in place we would have known that Nawaf al-Hazmi and Khalid al-Mihdhar, two of the muscle guys on the plane planning to hit the Pentagon, were in San Diego."

Completing the two-person "pro" team on the debate stage was celebrated legal scholar, trial lawyer, and civil liberties champion professor Alan Dershowitz. Why would one of the most prominent civil libertarians of our time chose to argue that state surveillance is a legitimate defence of our freedoms? For Professor Dershowitz the debate is not one of absolutes. As he argued throughout the two-hour contest, the challenge at hand is striking a balance, enshrined in law and overseen by the courts and Congress, between the privacy rights of individuals and the immense advantage surveillance programs give democratic societies facing complex, unconventional, and sophisticated terrorist threats. He believes our courts, democratic legislatures, and public servants are up to this challenge and that accountable, measured, and legally rigorous state surveillance is a necessary and achievable goal: "I sincerely believe that surveillance, properly conducted and properly limited, can really and genuinely protect our liberties. No state has ever survived without surveillance, and no state deserves to survive if it has too much surveillance, particularly against its own citizens. A balance has to be struck, but that balance cannot eliminate the power of government to obtain information necessary to the defence of our freedoms."

One formidable team of debaters deserves another, and here the Munk Debate on state surveillance did not disappoint. Arguing that state surveillance is not a legitimate defence of our freedoms was Glenn Greenwald, the investigative journalist at the centre of the Edward Snowden leaks that exposed America's "surveillance state" to the world. Greenwald is currently a columnist and lead writer for *The Intercept*, an online clearing house for Snowden's trove of data on the U.S. National Security Agency. He has been lauded by the *Financial Times* as the "most famous journalist of his generation," and *Foreign Policy* magazine singled him out as one of their 100 Leading Global Thinkers for 2013. Throughout the debate Glenn Greenwald demonstrated his trademark fluency with the legal, technological, and historical intricacies of mass surveillance programs in the United States and around the world. A passionate advocate for the sanctity of privacy rights in the face of corporate and state encroachment, Glenn Greenwald used the debate to paint a dark picture of a pervasive surveillance bureaucracy operating with little if any substantial legal or civilian oversight in the United States, Canada, and the United Kingdom, all of which are relentlessly collecting massive amounts of electronic data about people's intimate lives and conversations for analysis and detection. Glenn Greenwald reiterated his belief that mass, Internet-based surveillance of individuals was especially pernicious and that its effects on freedom of speech and freedom of assembly would prove chilling: "Over and over in the documents of the NSA we find not these mild paeans about the need for targeted surveillance, but the opposite. It is aggressive, boasting about the system of indiscriminate, suspicionless surveillance that they have constructed in the dark. Entire populations, hundreds of millions of people who are guilty of nothing, have their communications routinely monitored, surveilled, and stored."

The second debater arguing against the resolution brought his own unique perspective to the contest as a serial technology entrepreneur and fervent believer in the social goods that flow from an open and progressive Internet. Alexis Ohanian is the co-founder of reddit, the social news website used by 100 million people each month. For two years in a row he has been named to *Forbes'* prestigious "30 under 30: Technology" list.

Alexis Ohanian's contribution to the debate was to make the case for how widespread state surveillance affects the Internet itself and could threaten many of the characteristics of the World Wide Web that make it a transformative force for good in societies large and small. To quote Alexis Ohanian in his opening statement: "I could never have started reddit with the hope of it becoming a truly global platform if we thought we didn't have access to everyone with an Internet connection. The Internet works better the more people that are on it. But intelligence agencies have created an environment that is increasingly insecure for users, with the purpose of hopefully being able to take advantage of these security flaws for surveillance somewhere down the road."

Whatever preconceived notions anyone may have about this debate, readers will find the battle of wits between Michael Hayden, Glenn Greenwald, Alan Dershowitz, and Alexis Ohanian a refreshingly accessible and sophisticated exploration of whether or not state surveillance is in our collective interest. An analysis of the debate as a whole reveals that the state of public trust stands out as the key issue that animated our contest and what ultimately nudges opinion into either the "pro" or "con" camp. Do we trust that the systems of checks and balances built into our legislatures, courts, and bureaucracies (civil and military) are up to the task of managing and deploying the awesome technological powers of electronic state surveillance for our collective safety and benefit? Or is the very existence of mass government systems for data collection and analysis itself a corrosive social phenomenon, seeping through the body politic and eroding the trust between individuals and governments required to sustain the expectation of privacy in our technological age? The reading of this debate in its entirety and the companion interviews with each of the four protagonists will not definitively answer these questions, but they will, without a doubt, get you thinking about the swirl of issues and ideas that surround the debate over state surveillance in new and unexpected ways.

Rudyard Griffiths
Organizer and Moderator, The Munk Debates
Toronto, Ontario

Does State Spying Make Us Safer?

Pro: Michael Hayden and Alan Dershowitz
Con: Glenn Greenwald and Alexis Ohanian

May 2, 2014
Toronto, Ontario

THE MUNK DEBATE ON MASS SURVEILLANCE

RUDYARD GRIFFITHS: Ladies and gentlemen, welcome. Welcome to this extraordinary debate on state surveillance. My name is Rudyard Griffiths, and it's my privilege to act as the organizer of this semi-annual series and to once again serve as your moderator.

I want to start tonight's proceedings by welcoming the North America–wide television and radio audience tuning into this debate, everywhere from the Canadian Broadcasting Corporation (CBC) to CPAC, Canada's public affairs channel, to C-SPAN across the continental United States. A warm hello also to the thousands of people watching this debate live online on *The Intercept* and the Munk Debates web sites. It's terrific to have you as virtual participants in tonight's proceedings. And finally, hello to you, the over three thousand people who have once again filled Roy Thomson Hall to capacity for a Munk Debate. We thank you for your enthusiasm for the goal to which this series is dedicated: bringing big thinkers together to debate the big issues transforming Canada and the world.

The presence of the four outstanding thinkers on this stage momentarily to discuss the topic of state surveillance would not be possible without the generosity of our hosts for the evening. Please join me in showing our appreciation for the Aurea Foundation and its co-founders, Peter and Melanie Munk.

Now for the moment we've all been waiting for. Let's get our debaters out on stage and our debate underway. Speaking for the motion, "Be it resolved: state surveillance is a legitimate defence of our freedoms," is acclaimed trial lawyer, Harvard scholar, and storied civil libertarian, Professor Alan Dershowitz. Joining Professor Dershowitz on the pro side of tonight's debate is none other than Michael Hayden, the former head of the National Security Agency and the former head of the Central Intelligence Agency. He's also a retired four-star U.S. general.

Now, one great team of debaters deserves another, and we have not let you down tonight. Ladies and gentlemen, please welcome serial technology entrepreneur, the co-founder of the global social news phenomenon reddit and bestselling author, Alexis Ohanian. Alexis's partner tonight is a person who has been at the very centre of this global debate since Edward Snowden stunned the world last June with his unprecedented exposé on America's

Internet cyber-espionage programs. In the ensuing year our presenter has become, in the words of the *Financial Times* of London, the most famous journalist of his generation, ladies and gentlemen, First Look Media's Glenn Greenwald.

But before I call on our debaters for their opening statements, I would like to go over a housekeeping point, which is important for those of you in the hall. When you see our dastardly countdown clock appear on the screens at the end of the allotted time for opening statements, rebuttals, and closing statements, please join me in a round of applause for our speakers. This is going to keep them on their toes and, of course, our debate on time.

Now, let's find out how all of you, the three thousand of you, voted at the outset of this evening's debate on the resolution, "Be it resolved: state surveillance is a legitimate defence of our freedoms." The results are: 33 percent agree, 46 percent disagree, and 21 percent are undecided. So, this debate is definitely in play. Our second question will help us figure out how many of the three thousand people in this hall are open to changing their vote in the next hour and a half. Let's have those numbers. Wow — 87 percent of this audience are open to changing their vote — a very flexible crowd. Only 13 percent of you are committed resolutely to the "pro" or the "con" side. Now it's time to see which one of these teams can sway public opinion.

As per convention, the "pro" side will speak first, with six minutes for each opening remark. General Hayden, the floor is yours.

MICHAEL HAYDEN: Thanks for the introduction and the warm welcome. After I read your morning newspaper and saw that Alan and I were identified as two of the most pernicious human beings on the planet, I just wasn't really sure how welcoming you would be.

State surveillance is a legitimate defence of our freedoms. We all know the answer to that — it depends. It depends on facts. It depends on the totality of circumstances in which we find ourselves. What kind of surveillance? For what kind of purposes? In what kind of state of danger? And that's why facts matter. In having this debate, in trying to decide whether *this* surveillance is a legitimate defence of our freedom, we really need to know exactly what *this* surveillance is. And I freely admit, it's hard. This stuff has been pushed out into the world in a way that is unclear. Sometimes it's been presented in a way that is just wrong.

Let me give you an example. Information was leaked into the public domain about a program called Boundless Informant. If I were thinking of names that would eventually become public, it is probably not one I would pick. It was a heat map of the world that showed the metadata events that the NSA had acquired in one way or another. And the map also revealed tens of millions of metadata events that NSA was getting from France, Spain, and Norway. So the story immediately became, "These guys are checking the call logs of a whole bunch of Europeans."

The reality of the story was that French, Spanish, and Norwegian intelligence services were providing the NSA with metadata that their respective services had collected in internationally recognized theatres of armed conflict, not in Europe. It was a team effort, but it got rolled out very much as an aggressive, individual effort on the part of the NSA. These situations are complicated and people often incorrectly assume the most ominous possible thing is happening behind closed doors.

Do you remember something called the PRISM program that allowed the NSA to access materials on Google, Yahoo, and Microsoft servers in the United States — materials affiliated with a legitimate intelligence target? It was described in the media as "the NSA is free-ranging on the servers of Google and Microsoft and Yahoo." It was portrayed as uncontrolled NSA exploration of this data, which was incredibly wrong. The *Washington Post* was one of the papers that presented it in that way, and they ended up correcting it on their web site several days later, without notifying people that the article had been changed.

But let's skip all that for now. Let's try to get to the hard truth and boil down what CSEC (Communications Security Establishment Canada) is doing here, what the NSA's doing across the lake, what the GCHQ (Government Communications Headquarters) is doing in Great Britain, and what the ASD (Australian Signals Directorate) is doing in Australia. Even then you've got a problem, because you're walking into a movie theatre late in the third reel and you're looking at a scene, a snapshot of the film, and you're saying, "Aha! The butler did it!" Actually, you need to go back and look at the whole movie. You need to see what went on before, because if you know what happened earlier you might have a different interpretation of what it is you think the butler is guilty of.

There are a few things that the NSA and all these other security organizations have tried to solve. One of them is the war with volume: How do you conduct signals and intelligence to keep you safe in a tsunami of global communications? The answer is bulk collection and metadata. Critics suggest the NSA is "mucking about in those global telecommunication grids that have your emails," but no one complained when the NSA was eavesdropping on Soviet strategic forces' microwave rocket signals. The more modern equivalent of those Soviet microwave signals are proliferator, terrorist, narco-trafficker, money-launderer emails, coexisting with yours and mine out there in Gmail. And if you want the NSA or CSEC to continue to keep you safe, it is going to involve jumping into the stream where your data is stored.

After 9/11, the enemy was inside my country. Even when the enemy wasn't in my country, his communications were, since most emails reside on servers in the United States. An email from a bad man in Pakistan communicating to a bad man in Yemen should not deserve constitutional protection. The PRISM program is what allowed us to access those emails and what allowed us to keep everyone safe. There's a lot more to talk about, but you're going to start clapping in about nine seconds, so I'm going to go back to the podium. Thank you.

RUDYARD GRIFFITHS: The commanding presence of a four-star general. It's bred in the bone. Alexis Ohanian, you are up next.

ALEXIS OHANIAN: Hello, Canada. Thanks for being here while there is a basketball game going on. I really applaud you.

Americans and Canadians have a long history of shared values. Neither one of us wants to take responsibility for Bieber! But Biebs notwithstanding, one of those values is a right to privacy. It's something encoded in our governments and in our societies. It's something fundamental to who we are. We balance privacy with security, but the technological leaps that we have made in the last couple of decades have enabled a surveillance state that is at odds with these very fundamental rights. The Internet has made my career possible, as an entrepreneur and an investor, but it's also enabled a surveillance state that is simply unacceptable.

State surveillance is a threat to us for three reasons: it is an economic threat, it is a technological threat, and finally, and somewhat paradoxically, it actually undermines security and makes us more vulnerable. Both of our countries having leading tech sectors that are huge draws for talent and money from all over the world. But Forrester Research has estimated that the U.S. tech sector alone stands to lose over $180 billion because our global user-base is thinking twice before signing up for our services. Companies are looking to servers in other countries where they know they still have integrity. I just finished visiting over seventy-seven universities across the United States and Canada, including the Universities of Toronto and Waterloo, and I got to meet with tech entrepreneurs who have every right to believe they can create the next Google. However, some of their future users might think twice about running that search query because they don't know which intelligence agency is using it — and that is a real cost.

There is national security in economic security, and that has been undermined by this mass surveillance. The NSA's insatiable appetite for data has polluted the network. As citizens, as companies, as governments — we all share this online network. But the very infrastructure of the Internet has been threatened and is no longer healthy.

From a technological standpoint, the World Wide Web only works if it is worldwide. And now we hear that countries like Germany and Brazil are talking about Balkanizing the Internet. Steve [Huffman] and I never could have started reddit with the hope of it becoming a truly global platform if we thought we didn't have access to everyone with an Internet connection. The Internet works better the more people that are on it. But intelligence agencies have created an environment that is increasingly insecure for users, with the purpose of hopefully being able to take advantage of these security flaws for surveillance somewhere down the road.

Let me put it another way: it is as though law enforcement found out that there was a flaw in every lock in every door in the city of Toronto and didn't tell anyone.

They kept it safe so that one day they could maybe use it to take advantage of some unsuspecting bad person. Now, the obvious problem with this premise is that there is nothing stopping some other bad actor from taking advantage of that very flaw in the system, except that we're not just talking about the city of Toronto, we're talking about the entire world. This is our online reality right now, and it's simply unacceptable. Counterterrorism is making us less secure, and that is a technological fact.

I don't believe this has to be a trade-off between privacy and security. I'm talking about the trade-off between security that works and security that doesn't. Instead of encouraging our government to leave these flaws open so that we can exploit them one day, we should be fixing them. If we were to invest even a fraction of those data-collection dollars into making the network more secure, we would also be making our governments, our free societies, more secure.

And that brings me to an interesting point. I was lucky enough to get my first modem as a teenager, and it changed my life. As a dorky kid in suburban Maryland, I was able to get online and expand my horizons. The Internet has enabled so much good, but it's also facilitated so much bad. In the last century, before the Internet, only a certain amount of direct surveillance was possible. The laws allowed for a strict, very specific type of direct surveillance, and technology was rather limited. There was only so much intelligence agencies could do.

Now, thanks to the Internet — and thanks to some poor decisions on the part of our governments — the laws are now much weaker and the technology is much stronger. Thanks to the Internet, it is now cheaper and easier than before to conduct *mass* surveillance on innocent citizens. And so, while the Internet must be defended — while the values we hold so dear in Canada and the United States must be protected — it must not be done at the cost of our security.

The Internet is a fundamentally global, democratic platform, and it must stay that way. It embodies all the values we love as citizens in a democracy, and we have not been good stewards of it. But now is the chance to change all that, and I hope you'll work with me and Glenn to vote against this motion. Thank you.

RUDYARD GRIFFITHS: Excellent remarks. Professor Dershowitz, your opening statement, please.

ALAN DERSHOWITZ: Thank you very much. I know some of you are wondering if I'm on the right side of this debate. I've devoted my life to protecting privacy and civil liberties, and yet I'm for this proposition. It is because I sincerely believe that surveillance, properly conducted and properly limited, can really and genuinely protect our liberties. No state has ever survived without surveillance, and no state deserves to survive if it has too much surveillance, particularly against its own citizens. A balance has to be struck, but that balance cannot eliminate the power of government to obtain information necessary to the defence of our freedoms.

A proper balance requires a proper process for deciding

when surveillance is justified, when the need for preventive intelligence is greater in any particular case than the need for privacy. And in striking that balance, it's important to distinguish among different types and degrees of surveillance. There's a considerable difference, for example, between street cameras that observe the external movements of people in public places and hidden microphones that can listen to what you are saying in your bedroom. There's a difference as well between accessing the content of phone calls and emails and cataloguing the externalities of such messages — to whom they were sent, and when they were sent.

There's also a considerable difference between surveilling our own citizens and surveilling foreigners, including foreign leaders, who are probably trying to listen in on our leaders' conversations. To fail to base our policies on these differences is to fail in the very act of governance, which requires nuance and calibration. Matters of degree are important, and differences in degree can distinguish pragmatic democracies that are genuinely seeking to protect their citizens against real harms from self-serving tyrannies that seek only to protect their leaders from accountability.

We will hear tonight that terrorism and the need to protect our citizens is only a pretext — that there are other motives, sinister motives, for why we collect this information. So I will challenge our renowned opponents to identify those motives. Why would the Obama administration have continued this policy of surveillance after being briefed? Was it because President Obama has some sinister motive that he won't tell anybody about for gathering information? Is he only using terrorism as a pretext, an excuse, the way the Nazis in Germany used the Reichstag fire as a way of suppressing civil liberties? I don't believe that, and I hope you won't either.

Motives matter, though they too are difficult to discern and are frequently mixed. Many who supported the surveillance conducted by the FBI [Federal Bureau of Investigation] against the Ku Klux Klan and other racist groups during the civil rights movement opposed the very same surveillance techniques when they were used years later against the Black Panthers. And many who now applaud the decision to illegally record private statements made by Donald Sterling to his mistress would express outrage if equally pernicious statements made in private by people they admire and respect were subject to public disclosure. "Privacy for me, but not for thee" is as common as it is cynically self-serving.

We ought to be concerned about surveillance. There is virtually nothing that is immune from the pervasive eyes, ears, and even noses of the new generation of Big Brothers. This is absolutely true. But the most dangerous approach to our liberties is the all-or-nothing one, proposed by radical proponents or opponents of all government surveillance. Those who oppose all surveillance are as dangerous to our liberties as those who uncritically support all surveillance.

We need to know what harms our enemies, external and internal, are plotting in order to prevent them from carrying out their plans. But we also need to impose constraints, and that is why process comes into play. We need a demanding process, but we need to make sure that the burden is realistically designed to strike a proper balance between two equally legitimate but competing values: the need for preventive intelligence to stop attacks against us, and the need to protect our privacy from those who place too high a value on security and too low a value on privacy.

I believe it is possible to strike that balance in a manner that protects our freedoms, and that is where our efforts should be directed. Surveillance, properly limited and appropriately conducted, can promote liberty, protect life, and help us defend our freedoms. Our enemies, especially those who target civilians, have one major advantage over us: they are not constrained by morality or legality.

We have an advantage over them, in addition to operating under the rule of law: we have developed, through hard work and extensive research, technological tools that allow us to monitor and prevent their unlawful and illegal actions. Such technological tools helped us break the German and the Japanese codes during the Second World War. They helped us defeat Fascism; they helped us during the Cold War. And they are helping us now in the hot war against terrorists who would bomb this theatre if they had the capacity to do so.

You're going to hear again that these are only excuses, and that terrorism is not really a serious problem, or that American policy is as terroristic as the policy of al Qaeda. I don't think you're going to accept that argument. We must not surrender our technological advantage. Instead, we must constrain it within the rule of law by constructing appropriate processes governing its use.

I urge you to vote against rejecting all state surveillance, properly regulated, as a legitimate defence of our freedoms. I urge you to vote yes. Thank you very much.

RUDYARD GRIFFITHS: You can tell a trial lawyer through and through, since he was right down to the final second there. Congratulations Alan, that was terrific. Glenn, you're going to get the last word in the opening statements. The next six minutes are yours.

GLENN GREENWALD: Good evening. So, I want to begin by doing something that I am very unlikely to do for the next hour and a half, which is to vehemently agree with something General Hayden said. What he said at the beginning is absolutely right: In order to assess the resolution that we are debating tonight — is state surveillance a legitimate defence of our freedoms? — the first, and I think most important, question to ask is "what is state surveillance?" If state surveillance were only about targeting the people — in a discriminating and focused way — who are plotting terrorist attacks against our country or other countries, or are otherwise planning harm, there would be no debate. There would be no controversy. We could all end right now and go home.

Professor Dershowitz referenced the sinister radicals who are opposed to all surveillance and never want the government to spy on anybody ever again. I've been writing about this topic for eight years, and I have never met a single person who believes that. That is a straw man fantasy that does not exist. Unfortunately, the actual system of state surveillance that the United States and its surveillance partners have constructed almost entirely in the dark has almost nothing to do with this idea. It is not what Professor Dershowitz spent the last six minutes defending, which is focused surveillance designed to protect us from people who want to blow up the auditorium. If that were the case, there would be nothing to debate.

State surveillance is best understood by reviewing the NSA's own documents and own words, which, as I think you know, I happen to have a lot of. The phrase that appears over and over again to describe the system of surveillance they've constructed is "collect it all." The U.S. government, its officials, and defenders, like General Hayden, have become extremely adept — because of the secrecy behind which they operate — at presenting this very mild, pleasant, moderate picture about what it is that they do when they talk in public about these surveillance programs.

Unfortunately, those descriptions are wildly disparate from what they actually do and what they actually say in private when they think nobody's watching them. Over and over in the documents of the NSA we find not these mild paeans about the need for targeted surveillance but the opposite. It is aggressive, boasting about the system of indiscriminate, suspicionless surveillance that they have constructed in the dark. Entire populations, hundreds of millions of people who are guilty of nothing, have their communications routinely monitored, surveilled, and stored.

There's one particular document that I find incredibly striking, which was presented by the NSA in November 2011 at a signals development conference. The document is entitled, "Our New Collection Posture," and it says, in a chart, "Collect it all, snip it all, know it all, process it all, exploit it all."

In December 2013, a federal court judge in the United States, who was a George Bush appointee and a right-wing, pro–national security federal judge, ruled that the NSA data collection is a profound violation of the rights of millions of Americans. He described this program as "the almost Orwellian technology that is unlike anything that could have been conceived in 1979." William Denny, a mathematician with the NSA for thirty years who resigned in protest over what the NSA has become, told *Democracy Now!* in 2012: "They've assembled on the order of 20 trillion transactions between U.S. citizens and other U.S. citizens."

Before Edward Snowden even emerged, the *Washington Post* reported in 2011 that the NSA was collecting 1.7 billion emails and telephone calls every single day simply between and among American citizens, let alone what they collect on foreign nationals. *That* is the surveillance state that we are here to debate. It is unlike anything even science fiction writers in the 1950s could conceive of, and it is the opposite of the limited and focused program that our opponents are attempting to convince you exists.

I just want to make one point before my time is up about something Professor Dershowitz asked, which is, what is the reason for bulk collection? And of course they need a reason, because as citizens I think we all understand the inherent inappropriateness of having the government monitor and collect data about all of its citizens. And so the answer that they give over and over again — that my opponents are going to reiterate tonight over and over again — is one word: terrorism. They use that word because it packs a very powerful emotional punch. Professor Dershowitz will argue that those who claim terrorism is a pretext are just conspiracy theorists, but the U.S. government has used terrorism as a pretext for everything it has done in the past twelve years, from erecting a torture regime, to invading and destroying Iraq, to imprisoning people without charges in Guantanamo, to collecting the communications of all citizens throughout the globe, including its own. You don't need to be a conspiracy buff to think that is a pretext — you just require a basic knowledge of history. Even U.S. courts and government institutions over the last year have agreed and said these programs have nothing to do with terrorism.

RUDYARD GRIFFITHS: Ladies and gentlemen, four very formidable debaters! What talent on the stage tonight. We're going to allow them to extend their arguments a little bit further now with two-minute rebuttals, where they can weigh in on what they've heard from their opponents. We're going to ask the pro team to go first as a pair. General Hayden, you spoke at the top of the debate, so let's hear your rebuttal now.

MICHAEL HAYDEN: Two minutes is not enough time to unpack all the inaccuracies of the last twenty-four. Alexis, I actually agree with a lot of what you said. The Balkanization of the Internet would be a human tragedy. I agree that the American technology industry has suffered because of the stories that some people have written, but American industry is doing nothing more than what industries around the world are doing for their own intelligence services, and American industry is being unfairly singled out and punished because of it. However, I think you need to define the surveillance state.

Glenn, I don't agree with anything you said. You say that we collect everything there is — we do bulk collection, which is different than mass surveillance. The NSA collects .00004 percent of global Internet traffic. I have no idea what the 1.7 billion intra-American email collection that you were talking about means; it is simply not happening. What we have here are people trying to keep you safe. I've got an image in my head that you think the people who work and lead the NSA are like Mr. Burns from *The Simpsons* who maliciously say "excellent" while they spy on civilians.

RUDYARD GRIFFITHS: Extra points at the Munk Debates for any *Simpsons* references. Alan Dershowitz, your rebuttal.

ALAN DERSHOWITZ: I think we've heard two straw men from the other side. The first straw man is raising the issue of torture and rendition. I'm a liberal Democrat who voted against President Bush and who voted *for* Obama. I hate torture, I hate rendition — I'm against all of it. But does anyone doubt that all of that was motivated genuinely, if erroneously, by a desire to stop terrorism? Do you think that President Bush ordered these horrible things to be done just because he likes torture or likes rendition? He may have been wrong, but his motive, his goal, his purpose was to stop terrorism. So let's debate the merits of whether surveillance is good or bad, not what the motives are behind it.

The real straw man I heard from the other side was that we should just focus on terrorists. If only we could live in a world like that. If you could figure out a way to identify terrorists and only terrorists without the need to sometimes intrude on the conversation of somebody who might be talking to a terrorist, or who might know somebody who is a terrorist, I would be thrilled. But it is in the nature of life that one has to over-predict. We all know that when it comes to guilt or innocence and punishment, better ten guilty go free than one innocent be wrongly confined. But that is not the rule for preventive intelligence.

When it comes to preventive intelligence, it is far better that a few people have some intrusion than have one innocent person die because of an act of terrorism. We have to over-predict. We have to overuse. The question is, how much? How do we control it? How do we constrain it? I think we can have a lot of surveillance and still be consistent with liberty.

RUDYARD GRIFFITHS: Thank you. Glenn, let's have you up next and then Alexis will close out your side.

GLENN GREENWALD: On the question of motive: I actually don't care at all about it, primarily because I don't think I or anyone else can define it. I don't know why George Bush and General Hayden and the other officials in the United States invaded Iraq and destroyed the country, or why they tortured people, or why they put people in prison without charges. I only know that it was incredibly wrong to do, and that I feel the same way about surveillance. I bring it up because it all falls in the same sphere: the idea that if you say the word *terrorism* enough times you can put fear in people and justify whatever it is you want to do.

As far as whether or not this surveillance is actually about terrorism, let me share with you what people inside the U.S. government have said on that question so that you don't have to take either our word for it or the opposite side's. The federal court I referenced earlier, the one that ruled that the NSA was violating the rights of Americans, said, "The government does not cite a single case in which analysis of the NSA's bulk metadata collection actually stopped a terrorist attack." On December 18, 2013, a presidentially appointed panel composed of President Obama's closest aides issued a report that stated the following: "Our view suggests that the information contributing to terrorism investigations by the use of metadata was not essential to preventing attacks and could readily have been attained in a timely manner using conventional court orders." This is how I would like to respond to Professor Dershowitz about how else we can target people and find out what we need to know.

Three Democratic senators in President Obama's own party who are on the Intelligence Committee and have access to all classified information wrote a *New York Times* op-ed piece on November 25, 2013, in which they said, "The usefulness of the collection process has been greatly exaggerated. We have yet to see any proof that it provides real, unique value in protecting national security."

They hope that they will blind you with emotion, and I hope that you will focus on the evidence and the facts.

ALEXIS OHANIAN: Now it's my turn, right? Bring in the nerds. General Hayden, I'm happy that we're at least in accord on the technological costs of all of this surveillance. But I didn't hear a rebuttal about the real technological problems: the fact that the mass surveillance we are doing actually makes us less safe and less secure, which is something that we as Canadians and Americans have every reason to be worried about. We should be working to make the Internet stronger, to make it more secure, because it benefits all of us.

Our nations have been founded on principles that cherish things like a right to privacy and a right to freedom.

So what we're offering you here is this: the surveillance state has run amok. Technology that has enabled us to send selfies 24/7 has also enabled us to be spied upon 24/7. There is a way for due process. It was good enough for centuries before we had this technological innovation, and there is still a method to rein in this madness. But it starts by making the network more secure and not by making the average Canadian or American wonder who's listening and who's watching.

This is not the America I was raised in, and that's not the Canada I presume you all were raised in, and I hope that with all of us together we can make this right. Thank you.

RUDYARD GRIFFITHS: The battle lines in this debate could not be clearer. Now we're going to move on to our cross-examination period where we're going to get these two teams of debaters to engage with each other directly. I want to start with a question that I think comes out of the real points of contention here in the opening part of this debate: What are the risks that we are defending ourselves against by virtue of having these programs? General Hayden, you were running the NSA on September 11. If the current surveillance programs had been in place back then, could you have stopped that attack? I think that is the big litmus test on a lot of people's minds.

MICHAEL HAYDEN: First of all, let me point out that this isn't just about terrorism. This is about legitimate foreign intelligence activity to keep people safe and free. Terrorism is a big deal, but we do this for lots of good, legitimate reasons. To answer your question: if this metadata program — which *is* about terrorism, because the only reason you can use metadata is to stop terror attacks, no other purpose — had been in place we would have known that Nawaf al-Hazmi and Khalid al-Mihdhar, two of the muscle guys on the plane planning to hit the Pentagon, were in San Diego. They had been at a meeting in Kuala Lumpur and we had lost lock on them there — shame on us. I wish we had kept it. But then they came to the United States, unbeknownst to us, and the NSA actually intercepted their phone calls from San Diego, where they were staying, back to a known al Qaeda safe house in Yemen. We listened in.

We were listening to that particular phone call because we were covering the safe house in Yemen. As the call was being made, the NSA selection devices saw the number of the house in Yemen and we listened to the call a little more than half a dozen times. Nothing in the content of the call, nothing in the physics of the intercept, told us that the other end of the call was in San Diego. They didn't say anything in the call like, "Love the weather, the fleet's in, or we're going to the zoo tomorrow," which would have suggested they were in the California city.

If we had the 215 program at the time, we would have thrown that selector at that mass of American phone bills and phone connections and said, "Did anybody in here talk to this number in Yemen?" And ka-jing! The

San Diego number would have popped up. Now there's a lot the NSA can do with that. We would have handed that number to the FBI. The FBI would have kicked in the door in San Diego and would have found Nawaf al-Hazmi and Khalid al-Mihdhar, two people legally allowed in the United States. They probably would have leaned on them enough and found some reason to push them out of the country, and off they would have gone. And so two of the muscle guys on the Pentagon flight wouldn't have been there. I suspect al Qaeda would have maybe called off the raid, thinking, "We don't know what these guys gave up to the FBI; we don't know what else the Americans know. If they found these two guys, maybe they're lying in wait?" I'm guessing that would have happened.

RUDYARD GRIFFITHS: Thank you. So, Glenn, it sounds kind of convincing.

GLENN GREENWALD: Well, I have a lot to say about that, although I will try and make my remarks actually brief. I understand why General Hayden wants to claim that he didn't have the capabilities to stop 9/11. He was the head of the NSA at the time the 9/11 attacks took place and wants to suggest that he didn't have the ability to stop it. But that claim, which is incredibly inflammatory to Americans and to people throughout the world and the West — that we could have stopped 9/11 or disrupted this plot if we had the NSA programs that are in place now — has offended *the* leading experts on al Qaeda in the United States, who almost always defend the United States in the war on terror. Peter Bergen, who is one of them, wrote about this allegation for CNN on December 30, 2013: "Is it really the case that the U.S. intelligence community didn't have the dots in the lead-up to 9/11? Hardly. The failure to respond to these warnings was a policy failure by the Bush administration, not an intelligence failure by the U.S. intelligence community."

Lawrence Wright, the other expert, who wrote the Pulitzer Prize–winning and definitive book on al Qaeda in 2003, similarly wrote in the *New Yorker* in 2014 that 9/11 happened because the intelligence community had collected so much information that they had no idea what they were collecting and therefore didn't share the facts with each other that could have stopped the plot.

Their main problem right now is that they collect so much that they can't even physically store it all, even though you can store gargantuan information on a small little drive. When you collect that much, it's impossible to know and to detect when somebody is plotting to attack the Boston Marathon, or to blow up a plane, because they are collecting everything about all of us rather than only information about the people that they should be keeping their eyes on.

RUDYARD GRIFFITHS: Alexis, you're the tech expert, so I'd like to hear your opinion on this issue. Are we buried in data? General Hayden is saying that is precisely the challenge — there is too much data. We have to respond to it; we have to systematize it; we have to drill down into it. Are you just saying the technology is overwhelmed by the data itself?

ALEXIS OHANIAN: Yes. This is a very, very hard problem to solve. I mean, the gift and the curse of all the data, aside from the civil liberty violations, is that there may be some signal in there but there's a lot of noise. It's a very hard software dilemma to resolve. And that's only part of the problem, right, because through the efforts of this mass surveillance we've also undermined so much of the technology that makes the Internet work, and that keeps everyone of us safe. It becomes more than just an offensive use of surveillance on innocent civilians. It threatens the technology that allows the Internet to work well.

RUDYARD GRIFFITHS: Professor Dershowitz, come on in on this one.

ALAN DERSHOWITZ: Intelligence in the context of newly developing technology is always a work in progress. I think we're asking for too much right now, which is why motive is so important. And that is why it is so important to understand that Mr. Greenwald has conceded his major argument. He initially said that this is all a pretext, but now he says, "I don't care about motive." But pretext is all about motive. If you are prepared to concede that the motives are good and that it is a work in progress, we have to work to make it better. Greenwald wouldn't want to do this, though, because he says it's a pretext, and if it's a pretext then there is no use in trying to make it any better. I argue that it is well intentioned and well motivated, albeit with problems — there is too much information and too much gathering. I don't believe we are always gathering the right information, which is why we need to reform the Foreign Intelligence Surveillance Court [FISA Court], and that's why we need to have a range of other changes that allow us to take this work in progress and make it fit in a nice way into our war against terrorism without diminishing civil liberties. I think we can do it. We've done it with other technologies in the past. Let's not throw out the baby with the bathwater. Let's not restrict ourselves from using the tremendous technological advantage that we have worked so hard to achieve. Let's work to strike the appropriate balance.

RUDYARD GRIFFITHS: Glenn, can you see a policy where bulk data exists that strikes the right balance?

GLENN GREENWALD: No. Bulk data means indiscriminate mass collection — they are keeping track of who it is that you're talking to, who's calling you, and who is emailing you. And a legitimate government has no business monitoring and surveilling entire populations who are guilty of absolutely nothing. There is an attempt to suggest that there are different kinds of surveillance, and that it is okay to listen to phone calls or read emails, and to collect metadata. But when they say "just metadata," what does that mean? There are all kinds of studies, including from Professor Edward Felten at Princeton who has demonstrated that collection of your metadata can actually be more invasive than reading your emails or listening to your phone calls.

Imagine if you were to call an abortion clinic, or an HIV specialist, or a drug addiction or suicide hotline, or if you were to call someone who wasn't your spouse repeatedly late at night. Why should General Hayden and all of the national security state officials and your government and mine know that I'm calling those people so that they can use that however they wish? I do think that is illegitimate.

What is legitimate is to have targeted, focused surveillance on people who the courts have determined are actually guilty of some wrongdoing. It worked to keep us safe when the Soviet Union had massive intercontinental ballistic missiles pointed at every one of our major cities. It can certainly work to keep us safe from a few thousand people hiding in some caves.

RUDYARD GRIFFITHS: General Hayden, in interviews and elsewhere you have said that there is a fundamental difference between collection and surveillance, that these are two different activities.

MICHAEL HAYDEN: Yes, there is a difference between massive surveillance and bulk collection. Let me piggyback on a thought that Glenn put out there. He just suggested that the way we conducted surveillance against a slow-moving, oligarchic, technologically inferior — but incredibly dangerous — nation-state is the way we should protect civilians against a nimble, agile, fanatical, individually motivated, low-threshold (in terms of ability to detect) militant group. We cannot attack new threats the same way we attacked old ones.

Now, back to the metadata where I'm going to find out who is calling an abortion clinic. I started out by saying facts that matter, so I assume we're talking about the 215 program, all right? Because frankly, that is the only bulk metadata the NSA has on American citizens —

GLENN GREENWALD: And Canadians, too.

MICHAEL HAYDEN: We'll talk about foreign nationals —

GLENN GREENWALD: We should talk about everybody, especially in this room. They're all foreign nationals.

MICHAEL HAYDEN: The NSA gets the billing records of American citizens from American telephone providers. What happens to the billing records is actually really important. I didn't make this phrase up but I'm going to use it: they're put in a lockbox at the NSA. Twenty-two people at NSA are allowed to access that lockbox. The NSA is only allowed access to this truly massive data field when they have what is called a seed number. Imagine, for a second, what happens when they believe they have a seed number that is affiliated with al Qaeda. Someone rolls up to a safe house in Yemen with a phone we've never seen before. The NSA wonders if this phone might be associated with any threats in the United States?

So now — and I'm being a little cartoonish about this — the NSA gets to walk up to the transom and yell, "Anybody here talk to this number I just found in Yemen?" And then a number in Buffalo, for example, says, "I call him about every Thursday." The NSA gets to respond, "Okay, Buffalo number — by the way, number, not name — who did you call?" At which point, my description of the 215 metadata program is over — that is all NSA is allowed to do with the data. There is no data mining; there are no powerful algorithms chugging through it, trying to imagine relationships. It's "did that dirty number call someone in the United States?" The last year for which NSA had full records is 2012, but in that year, the NSA walked up to that transom and yelled, "Hey, anybody talk to this number?" 288 times. Now, that still may offend you, but that is not what was described over there [he points to his opponents].

RUDYARD GRIFFITHS: Alexis, let's have your opinion on that. What he has described is a fairly minimalist system. Others have described something that is pretty maximalist and pretty scary. Who's right?

ALEXIS OHANIAN: As a technologist I'm telling you yes, that metadata poses a very serious threat to us, because it is simply being gobbled up, sucked up, without any concern for due process, without any concern for the Fourth Amendment of the United States, without any concern for our right to privacy. And in aggregate, yes, it is far more surveillance than is necessary or required to do that job. I can't help but wonder who watches the watchers? Are we just basing everything on trust? I don't believe that's good enough, because in democracies we rely on transparency. We rely on knowing what is going on, and for too long we've had no knowledge of exactly what was going on. At the end of the day I think we all agree we want security above all, but the actions intelligence agencies have been taking through mass surveillance are in fact making us less secure.

RUDYARD GRIFFITHS: So, Alan, the middle ground between these two points exists. The government right now may be, as you think, benign, but what about some government in the future? What happens to this capacity not today but tomorrow? What about ten or twenty years from now?

ALAN DERSHOWITZ: James Madison said that if men or women were angels we wouldn't need the Bill of Rights. And we need the Bill of Rights because we don't trust government. This is why we need to impose constraints and why we need to have warrant requirements. We need to limit the ability to use these warrants and to use these surveillance methods.

But I think there is one big fundamental difference here. I think the "con" side assumes you can only surveil people who are guilty, but let me give you an example that I'm sure occurs right here in Toronto. It certainly occurs in London and New York. Among the new primitive technologies, we now have silent cameras on street corners, which has had a major impact on reducing street crime. Now, those cameras capture images of innocent people, all of us, walking along the street and doing our own thing. It doesn't capture what we say but it watches us. It's Big Brother. It's Big Brother writ small, perhaps, and it doesn't focus only on the guilty because criminals don't walk around with big *C*'s on their heads. We have these cameras in order to send a message to criminals that if you commit a crime, there will be a video footage and you will be captured. That has a big impact.

So you don't have to be guilty in order to surrender a little bit of your autonomy and privacy in the interests of preventing major crimes. So we ought to understand that we live on a continuum — a continuum of dangers, a continuum of rights violations. Not all rights violations are equal. Having yourself monitored walking through Times Square is, as I said in my opening, very different from having the government listen to what you say in your bedroom. And that's the kind of debate we should be having — not one about innocence or guilt.

Due process is very nimble and very flexible. It is the process that is due to you, based on the degree of intrusion compared to the degree of benefit the government gets out of it. That is the way we ought to have this debate. We ought not to end all surveillance and all intrusions. Although Mr. Greenwald keeps denying this, when you really listen closely to what he is saying, he really sounds like he is against all surveillance unless you can find a guy with the al Qaeda card, wearing an al Qaeda uniform and baseball hat. And if you can't pinpoint and identify him with 100 percent certainty, don't you ever dare to try to find him by intruding even slightly on the privacy interests of innocent people. That is not the way government works, nor should it work that way.

GLENN GREENWALD: You know, I completely understand why Professor Dershowitz wants to attribute these positions to me that are completely laughable and ridiculous, because it is so much easier to debate people when you can pretend they hold moronic views that they don't actually believe. If I believed what he just said I believe, I would urge you to vote against me. However, I don't think any of it.

There is a process that has been in place from the time the United States was telling the world that the Soviet Union was this evil empire and was the greatest threat known to man, a process that all presidents, Democrat and Republican alike, understood was the way to keep America safe. They followed a procedure of going to court and getting a warrant before they were given permission to watch somebody and listen to their phone calls. They didn't have to present definitive proof-positive evidence that the people they were surveilling were guilty of something, but they had to present enough reasonable cause so that there were safeguards over who was being monitored. It also gave intelligence agencies enough of an ability to then listen and see whether or not there was cause to believe they should continue to be surveilled —

ALAN DERSHOWITZ: Would you require a warrant for that camera on the street that I spoke about earlier?

GLENN GREENWALD: No, and I want to explain why. Watching people on a street camera is fundamentally different than watching what people do online. The Internet is not simply a place that you pass by on the street, which I think is one of the reasons why younger people have been so supportive of Edward Snowden and view him as a hero. The Internet is a place where we explore who we are as human beings — it's where we make our friends, it's where we read, it's where we think. It is everything about who we are.

To remove all the privacy from the Internet, a space where we exist and grow and explore, through this collect-it-all mentality is a kind of privacy invasion unlike any that has ever taken place. Let me leave you with one quote from James Bamford, an NSA historian who has worked on these issues for a long time. He said that granting the NSA the ability to invade people's online activity allows them to invade people's minds, people's thoughts, and their very person. I think we all understand the value of privacy, even those of you who voted yes on this resolution at the very beginning of the evening. I can guarantee you all put passwords on your email and social media accounts and lock your bedroom and bathroom doors. You wouldn't want me or General

Hayden or anyone else trolling through it, because as human beings we all understand that privacy is a unique guarantee of human freedom — it's where creativity and dissent and exploration reside, and when that is gone so, too, is a crucial part of human freedom.

RUDYARD GRIFFITHS: That is the perfect segue to watch a video that was created especially for tonight's Munk Debate. It touches on what the Internet means and how surveillance impacts it. Ladies and gentlemen, please listen to Edward Snowden in this exclusive video.

EDWARD SNOWDEN: Hello, and thank you for inviting me to speak to you tonight. I'm sorry I couldn't be there in person.

State surveillance today is a euphemism for mass surveillance. The problem with this mass surveillance is that it is no longer based on the traditional practice of targeted taps based on some individual suspicion of wrongdoing, like thinking a person is a spy or terrorist. The traditional practice had natural limitations based on the high cost of maintaining taps, and the high risk of detection by targets if we used it too recklessly or too broadly. Those limitations ensured intrusive surveillance would only be used as a last resort, as a true necessity, when there were no other less intrusive means of getting the same information.

Today we've lost those limitations as a result of technological advances. State surveillance is now cheap, undetectable, pervasive, and available at the click of a mouse. As a result, entire populations rather than individuals live under constant surveillance, which happens as a matter of convenience to the intelligence community rather than as a result of true necessity in preventing harm. These are facts, not allegations. For example, the *Washington Post* confirmed that the NSA is now intercepting and recording every single phone call in entire countries, which is both metadata — the information about where the call originated and where it is answered, how long it is, and information about associations — and the voice and its content. The NSA records what those people said on the call and it is stored for a whole month even if the people are not suspected of any crime, any wrongdoing, or of causing any problems at all. So we have to ask ourselves: Is today's state surveillance — is mass surveillance and the monitoring of the private lives, of the hopes and dreams of every man, woman, and child in these countries — a legitimate defence of our rights?

Do we realize that these systems we are building, this technology that we are developing, can be targeted inward at any time? It already has been — at least for the metadata portion — by people in the room, including Michael Hayden, who, as head of the NSA, launched a program called Stellar Wind, a domestic, unconstitutional surveillance program that operated in the United States without any authorizing statute at all.

This is an idea of what today's state surveillance looks like, but it's important to remember that it doesn't stop with phone calls. It monitors your emails, your text messages, your Web history, every Google search you've ever made, and every plane ticket you've ever bought. They watch what books you buy at Amazon.com and where the transactions are sent in plain text. Anyone — whether it is the NSA or some other foreign intelligence service — can collect this information and store it for extended periods of time.

The surveillance includes knowing who your friends are and how you communicate with them. It shows where you go and what you want to be. It also shows people in charge of state surveillance who you love and where they live. Now, defenders of this kind of unconstitutional dragnet surveillance say there is no room for abuse because we have policies in place to address these concerns. But can policies that change with every new president, with every new congress, with every new director of the NSA really address the threat building inside our own country? Can they deal with this kind of architecture of oppression?

What about other countries that don't abide by our policies? Is leaving our communications insecure so that the NSA can monitor them and those of our adversaries really worth the cost? And we have to remember, the policies aren't perfect. As an NSA analyst, I had the authority to wiretap anyone without leaving my desk as long as they had a private email address, from a federal judge to the President of the United States — and that is not a boast.

Examples of abuse have already occurred. In 2009, the *New York Times* reported that we used our state surveillance infrastructure to improperly access Bill Clinton's email, and that NSA workers used surveillance to spy on their lovers, ex-girlfriends, and other individuals who were obviously not suspected of any kind of crime at all. It is important to note that none of those individuals were ever charged with crimes. Why are intelligence agency employees not held accountable when they break the law, abuse infrastructure, and lie to the American people?

I believe it is because in the calculus of state power your rights are worth less to the government than the continued secrecy and operation of these programs. The court battles invite scrutiny that the government simply doesn't want. Now, there are other far worse abuses that have yet to be reported. We need to understand that the NSA violates laws, regulations, and policies thousands of times per year.

While our opponents might say that we can trust that the NSA's massive surveillance of our private records can't be abused, last year demonstrated that any Booz Allen Hamilton contractor who doesn't even work for the government can take those private records and walk out the door with them. And if they hadn't gone to the press and returned that *public* information back to *public* hands, then no one would have ever known about it.

To conclude, I'd like to remind you that even if these state surveillance programs were perfect, even if they were never abused, and even if the oversight failures that are all too common today were fixed, these programs have never been shown to be uniquely valuable to keeping us safe. You don't have to take my word for it. Two independent White House panels with complete access to classified information found that these programs had never stopped a single imminent terrorist attack in the United States. One of them went further to say that these NSA operations had no basis in law at all. The first open court reviewing these programs called them Orwellian and unconstitutional. Congress is now working to pass the USA Freedom Act, which would end some of the most abusive programs entirely. I would argue that when all three branches of government agree that these programs should end, it seems clear to me that they are not a legitimate defence of our freedoms, but they are in fact a clear and present danger to them and to our way of life as Americans. Thank you very much for listening.

RUDYARD GRIFFITHS: That's a clip from a special seven-minute statement that Mr. Snowden recorded exclusively for the Munk Debates. The full video is available at www.munkdebates.com/snowden for those who want to have a look. Alan, I'd like to ask you about a number of points there that we've covered, especially accountability, which I think is key. Edward's claiming that he can log in to the president's email, not even as an NSA employee but as a contractor. To what degree do we have a system in place now that is powerful enough to harness this technology in the ways that you want to see it utilized?

ALAN DERSHOWITZ: I think General Hayden should answer that question, but I'd love to follow up afterwards.

MICHAEL HAYDEN: If Edward Snowden were able to do that, it would not only be a violation of the laws of the United States but it would also violate the laws of physics. Yes, he had access to the NSA's administrative network, but he did not have access — thank God — to the NSA's operational network. There's no one in the NSA who believes there is any possibility that he did what he claims to have done.

ALAN DERSHOWITZ: Let me follow up on that. The U.S. Supreme Court on Tuesday of this week heard one of the most important arguments that it will hear this year. The issue before the Supreme Court was that, under current rules, if I were to get arrested today for jaywalking or for driving my car without a seat belt, the police officer searching me could seize my iPhone and access all of its data, including my medical and tax records. This isn't the NSA — it is what happens when modern technology confronts the Fourth Amendment.

The Supreme Court heard the argument: out of nine justices, eight of them expressed their views and were deeply divided. I really urge you to read the transcript because it demonstrates how our Supreme Court works. You can tell that they were deeply confused, deeply troubled, and trying to figure out a way to apply the intentions of the framers (who wrote the Constitution in 1793 and couldn't imagine how technology would transform) and the words of the Fourth Amendment to this modern technology. And the Supreme Court doesn't write decisions only for today; the judges write them for the next year, the next decade, and for decades after that.

Again, this is all a work in progress. We are trying to get accountability. Technology is always ahead of the law. In my fifty years of teaching at Harvard, I've tried to teach my students not only how to practise law today but how to practise law when you're my age. It's always a quest. And to answer your question: we don't have enough accountability now, but we're getting there, and you can help us get there.

This is not only an American problem. The Five Eyes work together: the United States, Canada, New Zealand, Australia, and England. They share intelligence and information. You're not foreigners when it comes to your own government. Your government is trying to protect you as well, and your Supreme Court is also struggling with these issues. Don't make it a choice between good and evil, as Mr. Greenwald is framing it. There are good people struggling to do the right thing. Let's keep the struggle going but let's not throw out surveillance, which requires sometimes monitoring innocent people.

RUDYARD GRIFFITHS: Alan, we have to be conscious of equal time here, so let me bring Glenn in.

GLENN GREENWALD: I am going to begin by saying that U.S. national security officials are very adept and very skillful at presenting a public image that is wildly different than the reality. The whole NSA scandal began when James Clapper, the director of national intelligence, went before our Senate and said the NSA was not mass collecting data about millions of Americans. And then, the very next story that we reported from the Snowden archive two months later proved that the NSA was doing that exact thing, which the top national security official of the U.S. government falsely denied to the Senate and to the public. And so we hear things like "Mr. Snowden is not telling the truth when he says that he sat at his desk and could have wiretapped anyone," but I guarantee that is exactly what NSA analysts have the capability to do. And what evidence do we have? Don't rely on my word or Snowden's, just look at the XKeyscore program, which we reported in the *Guardian* in September 2013. The program has ample documents that show an analysts' training manual that outlines, in great detail, how to eavesdrop on a particular email. Nobody checks what you're doing. You simply start receiving those emails exactly as Mr. Snowden said.

And to the question of whether there are really any safeguards, Hayden said, "It's in a lockbox. We are collecting all your data, but don't worry it's very well protected." History proves that you cannot trust governments to collect information and not abuse it. Think about this fact: the NSA is an agency where Edward Snowden sat for many months and downloaded all of their most sensitive documents, and they had no idea he was doing it. To this day, they have no idea what he took, even though they spent tens of millions of dollars trying to figure it out. Does that sound like a very well-managed system to you? A system you can trust with all of your data?

One last point I want to make: Professor Dershowitz keeps returning to the issue of motive, which I have said from the beginning doesn't matter.

ALAN DERSHOWITZ: What does pretext mean, then?

GLENN GREENWALD: If somebody invaded Iraq because they were an evil person or were incredibly misguided and amoral, for example. Here's what I do know: in a recent interview, Professor Dershowitz said the NSA talks about the FISA Court as a form of oversight, but the FISA Court is pretty much a joke. It gives out warrants, as he said, like lollipops. Whatever the court's motives, the climate in the United States after 9/11 got out of control. I was in Manhattan on that day. I still remember the emotions it triggered, and it was a very traumatic event. And the balance that we always had or tried to maintain got completely out of whack — everything was justified in the name of terrorism, from destroying a country of 26 million people to putting people in prison without charges, to torturing them, to spying on everybody's emails and telephone calls. That is what is wrong, that is what is dangerous, and that is what I hope you'll reject tonight by voting against the motion.

RUDYARD GRIFFITHS: Before we go to closing statements I want to provide Alexis Ohanian an opportunity to reflect on Snowden's statement, on what came out of that statement. What do you think is the key point from his video?

ALEXIS OHANIAN: Like I said, I'm the nerd here. I still want to point to my opening remarks about the fact that what we are doing with mass surveillance actually undermines the strength and security of our nations, as well as oversteps the bounds and the rights of privacy that we all have. Remember that as Canadians and Americans our governments work for us: we hire them, sometimes fire them.

Technology does not grow linearly; it grows exponentially. We can do things in the last twenty years that we could not have even imagined in the twenty years prior. And a lot of these things are really great, but some are not. And one of the things that has run amok because of this technological boom is this surveillance state.

RUDYARD GRIFFITHS: It's now time for closing statements. We're going to give each of our debaters three minutes, and they are going to speak in the reverse order of the opening. So, Glenn, that means that you are up first.

GLENN GREENWALD: I feel like I anticipated one of the problems that this debate was going to entail, which is the ability of each side to make claims about the meaning of the surveillance state. Is it this nice, well-motivated work-in-progress where we just try to eavesdrop on the terrorists, but oh-so-accidentally, and just very occasionally, bump into your Gmail? Or is it what the NSA actually described it as being when they didn't know you were listening: "Collect it all, snip it all, process it all, know it all, exploit it all." Those are not my words; those are the words of the NSA working in a top-secret environment. Don't vote on Professor Dershowitz's aspirations for what he hopes state surveillance might do someday. The way we get to that point is by rejecting what it is now, which is excessive and menacing and dangerous.

The second point that I think is vital to make is one that Alexis just touched on, which is this now mockery over the idea that what kept us safe from the Soviet Union is simply woefully inadequate. If you go back and look at what was said by Ronald Reagan and world leaders in the '70s and '80s, it was that the Soviet Union was the greatest threat ever to mankind — we went to war to prevent them from doing what they wanted to do. Suddenly people have started saying: "Oh, those Soviets were nice, reasonable people who we could manage; it's really those terrorists in a cave who are forcing us to fundamentally dismantle our system of liberties so that we can protect ourselves."

General Hayden keeps asking for facts, and I think I've presented a lot of facts in this debate, but let me just leave you with a few more. In 2009 the global news service McClatchy characterized the threat of terrorism this way: "Undoubtedly more American citizens died overseas from traffic accidents or intestinal illnesses

47

than from terrorism." In March 2011, *Harper's* offered this statistic: "The number of American civilians who died worldwide in terrorist attacks last year, eight. The minimum number who died after being struck by lightning, twenty-nine." Terrorism is a real threat — it is not anything to make light of — but there are also all sorts of threats that we guard against and keep ourselves safe from that haven't required us to dismantle our fundamental liberties, like the right to privacy or loosening the limitations on the government's ability to know what we are saying. We need to balance these concerns with the values that we are trying to protect in the first place. Thank you.

RUDYARD GRIFFITHS: Professor Dershowitz, your closing statement.

ALAN DERSHOWITZ: I think we need less surveillance than what we have now, but more than what Mr. Greenwald and Mr. Ohanian want, which would require a warrant to specify the suspicion level against anybody whom we would surveil at all. We need a reasonable middle ground on which we can use some surveillance based on less-than-probable cause in order to target people who are trying to do harm to us.

Now, terrorism is real and it's different than viruses; it's different than being struck by lightning. It's an essential attack on the very core of our country and our people. I actually believe that one of the greatest threats that civil liberties face in this country would be another terrorist attack like 9/11. Even if fewer people were killed in traffic accidents, the devastating impact another attack like 9/11 would have on our civil liberties would be incalculable.

If you don't believe me, just think back to Canada in 1970, when two terrorist kidnappings resulted in the invocation of the War Measures Act, which deprived Canadians across the country of some of their basic civil liberties. I, along with Irwin Cotler, served as consultants to the Liberal prime minister Pierre Trudeau, and to the Liberal attorney general in those days — John Turner — to try and figure out a way of reducing the impact on civil liberties without diminishing the prevention of terrorism.

It's in the interest of every person who cares about liberty to take reasonable steps to prevent another mass-casualty attack. A surveillance system directed against terrorism and those facilitating terrorism — which will have false positives and will result in the intrusion on some privacy of some people who are innocent — is essential both to the defence of our citizens and to the protection of our liberties. I urge you to vote for this proposition and to allow our governments, all of the Five Eye governments — to work together to allow us to have the intelligence necessary to prevent a recurrence of 9/11.

Will it prevent it? Nobody knows for sure. Will it increase the likelihood of preventing it? I think we can be fairly assured that is the case. We need to improve our system of surveillance; we need not scrap it, because reasonable state surveillance is a legitimate defence of our freedoms.

Do not vote to tie our hands, to deprive us of an essential tool in the real war against real terrorism. Vote yes on this proposition if you want to see a proper balance struck between the legitimate need for surveillance and the equally legitimate need for privacy.

RUDYARD GRIFFITHS: Alexis, your three minutes.

ALEXIS OHANIAN: Thank you. Mr. Dershowitz, it sounds like we might be winning you over, at least with the idea of less surveillance.

Now look, technology has enabled so much. But with that technology we've enabled a surveillance state that is out of control. Fundamentally this is a problem because (1) it affects our economic strength, and economic strength is a vital part of our national security; (2) it affects the underpinnings of the very technology that makes the Internet work — the surveillance we're undertaking has a huge impact on data protection; and (3) it gives comfort to the leaders of countries that want to use the Internet to spy on their own citizens. But the most important point is that what we are doing in the name of security actually makes us less secure, and it makes us more vulnerable. Remember the example I gave of the key? That is the layperson's version of what we are doing with surveillance. We are finding flaws in the system and we are holding onto that key for ourselves, leaving every one of our homes vulnerable.

I am from a generation that can't imagine a world without the Internet, but I have a feeling most of you think the Internet has become pretty indispensable. It is the place where we go not only to start companies but also to have discussions, sometimes combative ones, to make new friends, to have relationships, to find that there are other people all over the world that have ideas we can benefit from and then remix and share. And all of those things are possible because we have a flat Internet. Sorry, Tom Friedman, while the world may not be flat, the World Wide Web is. Our nations have done so much to lead the way in innovation because every one of us as citizens believed that our private-most thoughts were safe and secure.

State surveillance is not acceptable in this Internet age because it can undo all this innovation. Technologically, this kind of surveillance was impossible in the past and laws made direct surveillance the only option. Today, the laws have been weakened and technology makes it cheap and easy to gobble up all that data from every single one of us. This is an unprecedented situation where surveillance disproportionately affects innocent people.

I know there are good people at the NSA trying to keep us safe; I know they have our best interests at heart. But I also know the surveillance state is full of people who are maybe too preoccupied with whether or not they *could*, but didn't stop to think about whether or not they *should*. Thank you.

RUDYARD GRIFFITHS: The final closing statement goes to you, General Hayden.

MICHAEL HAYDEN: I started out as "pernicious," and picked up "untruthful and untrustworthy" along the way. But apparently, as a former U.S. intelligence official I'm a good storyteller, so here it goes.

Talk about scare tactics! We need to run the tape and count how many times Alan and I said terrorism and how many times Glenn and Alexis said surveillance state. What do they really mean by surveillance state? The 1.7 billion U.S. emails that are collected a day? It can't be that because it's simply untrue. What is it you think we're doing? I love the Snowden quote: "It covers your text messages, your Web history, every search you've ever made." Guess what? That's Google, not the NSA.

After the Boston Marathon bombing, we discovered that the Tsarnaev kids had visited jihadist web sites before the attack. The American political leadership slapped around the security establishment with people asking, "How come you didn't know they went to jihadist web sites?" The answer is because we are not allowed to monitor the Internet activity of Americans, or Canadians, Australians, and New Zealanders either. What Glenn and Alex are describing simply isn't going on.

With regard to the Soviet Union and their threat level, I didn't say they were reasonable or safe, I just said their communications were on a dedicated isolated network, which creates a different dilemma.

With regard to oversight, Glenn mentions Judge Leon, who said that the program was "probably" unconstitutional. That makes Glenn's side one for thirty-seven in court decisions on the constitutionality of this matter. And, by the way, Judge Leon stayed his own decision.

The NSA's mantra "collect it all" doesn't mean collect it all. They'd drown in it all if they did, because they can't use it all. What it means is that they want the ability to cover any communications by any method, at any time — communications of those who would do you harm. Trust me, if what Glenn and Alexis say is true were true, and if what Alexis fears is true were true, I'd vote for them, too. Thank you.

RUDYARD GRIFFITHS: Well ladies and gentlemen, a superb debate on a complicated, important topic. Please give a big round of applause to these four gentlemen. Bravo. And a big thank you to our hosts tonight, the Aurea Foundation and Peter and Melanie Munk who, year after year, have tirelessly supported this debate. Thank you for this debate series.

Now for a crucial part of tonight's proceedings: Which one of these two teams has been able to sway opinion in this hall? Let's review where the vote stood at the beginning of the evening, before we listened to the last hour and forty minutes of debate and conversation. The numbers for the initial audience vote: 33 percent agreed with the motion, 46 percent disagreed, and 21 percent were undecided. We also wanted to know the percentage of you who would change your vote depending on what you heard: 87 percent said they were open to changing their vote.

For those of you in Roy Thomson Hall, you're going to get another paper ballot to choose yes or no on the resolution. Ladies and gentlemen, thank you for a marvellous debate. Let's see how it turned out.

Summary: The pre-debate vote was 33 percent in favour of the resolution, 46 percent against it, and 21 percent undecided. The final vote showed 41 percent in favour of the motion and 59 percent against. Given that more of the undecided votes shifted to the team arguing against the resolution, the victory goes to the team arguing against the resolution, Glenn Greenwald and Alexis Ohanian.

Pre-Debate Interviews
with Rudyard Griffiths

GLENN GREENWALD IN CONVERSATION
WITH RUDYARD GRIFFITHS

RUDYARD GRIFFITHS: My name is Rudyard Griffiths, and I am the moderator of the Munk Debates. I will be interviewing all of tonight's debaters in the next hour, starting with Glenn Greenwald, who is arguing against the resolution, "Be it resolved: state surveillance is a legitimate defence of our freedoms."

Glenn, terrific to have you here because you are an essential part of this debate. In fact, you and Edward Snowden have been at the centre of this global conversation over the last eleven months, and I bet it's been tough at times. I know there is going to be a lot to your argument, but what is the key point that you want to say to a skeptic out there who is suggesting that state surveillance might not be such a bad thing?

GLENN GREENWALD: I think the main question is, what do we mean by state surveillance? Nobody would dispute the validity of the state's surveillance of specific targets for whom there was credible evidence that they were engaged in plotting terrorist attacks or other violent or criminal activities. Unfortunately this idea has almost nothing to do with the actual system of state surveillance that has been implemented. It is not at all targeted or discriminating but is instead indiscriminate and even targets those who aren't suspected of criminal activity. It is a system where they put entire populations, hundreds of millions of people, under a surveillance microscope without regard for whether they've done anything wrong. It's the ubiquity of the system — the indiscriminate nature of it — that makes it so menacing.

RUDYARD GRIFFITHS: But what do you make of people who say that if you want to find a needle in a haystack, you need to have access to the whole haystack? It's optimistic to think that we could target one terrorist, but if we want to find out whom that terrorist talked to, and whom that person talked to, bulk collection is the way to go.

GLENN GREENWALD: We don't accept that way of thinking in any other context. If we were to tell people that we wanted to put monitors in their homes to watch what they are doing at all times simply because we want to find people committing crimes, the public would instinctively understand why that is repellent.

The other point I would refute about mass surveillance

is that it assumes rather falsely that it's efficient to find terrorists by monitoring everybody — the exact opposite is true. If you are collecting billions of telephone calls every single day, which is what the NSA and its partners are doing, it becomes almost impossible to find out who is actually plotting terrorist attacks. They've collected so much information on regular people it makes it difficult to identify radicals, those who support terrorist organizations, or the people who want to detonate a bomb on an airplane or plant a bomb at the Boston Marathon. It is completely inefficient.

Terrorism is the pretext but not the real reason for the surveillance system. We've exposed spying on Brazilian oil companies, economic conferences, which are held regionally, and all sorts of democratically elected governments that have nothing to do with terrorism. The United States uses terrorism as an excuse for almost everything it wants to do, and it is the excuse the government uses for the system of mass surveillance as well.

RUDYARD GRIFFITHS: Some of your critics at the NSA and elsewhere would say that you are conflating collection with surveillance. They argue that surveillance is only undertaken once they've sifted through all of the data and have got down to the few people they think are legitimate suspects — people that you would maybe also agree are bad guys — and that deserve a closer look. Do you think a distinction needs to be made between collection and surveillance?

GLENN GREENWALD: First of all, when the government stores the list of people with whom you are communicating, or stores your emails, or records your telephone conversations, that is surveillance in every sense of the word. Once your information is in the system, anyone who has access to that system, the tens of thousands of analysts and employees who work for both the U.S. government and private contractors have the ability to access it with virtually no oversight or supervision.

Secondly, history has proven that when you allow the government to collect that amount of information, inevitably it will be abused. People who the U.S. government perceives as being threats to national security are often nothing more than people who are effectively opposing its agenda.

RUDYARD GRIFFITHS: You've written that in addition to threatening privacy in America, you think the NSA and its programs are really, in a sense, out to destroy privacy as a global norm. Can you unpack that for us and explain the consequences?

GLENN GREENWALD: The NSA uses one simple but important phrase to describe what they are doing: "collect it all." Their institutional objective is the collection and storage of every single form of electronic communication that takes place by and between human beings. They want to eliminate the concept of privacy around the world by making every conversation and every electronic action susceptible to their surveillance systems.

They aren't just spying on Americans; the NSA is indiscriminately spying on the entire world. The Internet, once such a promise of liberation, liberalization, and democratization, instead becomes the greatest tool of coercion and suppression ever known to humanity. This is the NSA's goal and it is one that they are increasingly close to fulfilling.

RUDYARD GRIFFITHS: How do you respond to those who say that the United States is using a constitution written in the eighteenth century to define privacy, and that perhaps our privacy expectations need to catch up to 2014, which by implication may mean we should be more comfortable about sharing our data with the government if we believe that this makes us safer individually and collectively?

GLENN GREENWALD: A lot of these debates are actually quite old even though we feel as though they are new. The concept of general warrants was one of the principal motivations for why the former subjects of the British Crown, now known as Americans, waged an incredibly risky revolution — the idea that the king could subject entire communities to search and seizure. The state would enter homes, search for documents or other objects, hoping to find dangerous fugitives. The colonists believed it was completely legitimate for the state to do so if they got individual search warrants to prove that somebody had committed a crime.

Even though we know that, by putting that limit on

the state, lots of people are going to have an easier time committing crimes, and dangerous criminals and rapists and child molesters are going to evade capture, history has shown that we continue to vehemently resist the idea that generalized searches without sufficient proof are in any way a proper function of the state. The need to have a private realm is so critical to being a free person that nothing justifies allowing its invasion. The principle of privacy protection is every bit as valid today as it was during the American revolutionary period, except that it is actually more imperative now, because the Internet is not just a place where we send a letter, like a post office, or make a call the way we do with a telephone service. The Internet is the place where we store all of our data, where we engage in all kinds of transactions, and where we read and form who we are — all of which reveal the innermost workings of our minds. To convert such a comprehensive venue of culture, thinking, and individual exploration into a place of comprehensive surveillance is, I'd say, infinitely more dangerous than any of the prior controversies over surveillance in the past.

RUDYARD GRIFFITHS: Where do you think this debate is headed? You are sitting on a treasure trove of documents of which only a small percentage of the total has been released. Do you think this debate is going to burn itself out before we get to major reforms? Your own president, Barack Obama, seems to be soft-shoeing the idea of more substantial privacy reform and reining in entities like the NSA.

GLENN GREENWALD: I feel as though the interest in this story globally is as high and as intense as it was after the first week of our revelations simply because the revelations have continued. I don't think the outrage and shock over the disclosures have been in any way diluted in the United States or in the rest of the world.

The behaviour of politicians is often the best bellwether of public opinion. Just a month and a half ago, President Obama himself — after repeatedly defending the metadata bulk collection program in the United States — came out and called for its end. He said the U.S. government should not be in the business of collecting this data in bulk.

RUDYARD GRIFFITHS: But now the telecoms will hold that information for the government.

GLENN GREENWALD: I doubt very much they will. Obama wants to end the practice of having the government not only possess it, but also have access to it, except in very specific cases. I think the reason he's suggesting it and you see senate campaigns constructed around the need to place limits on the NSA is precisely because the lingering public awareness of the issue is quite acute. So, no, I don't think public interest in the stories are burning out. I think there are a lot of stories to come that will intensify that public interest in Canada, in the United States, and around the world. And I am extremely optimistic about the ability to sustain the interest level because of how important the Internet has become in people's lives.

RUDYARD GRIFFITHS: And finally, how is Edward Snowden? What is his state of mind? Does he have any plans to return to the United States?

GLENN GREENWALD: In general, he's doing great. When we were in Hong Kong working on these stories, our working assumption was that he was going to end up in the custody of the U.S. government sooner rather than later and be put into a cage for probably the next several decades as punishment for the disclosures he exposed. He is incredibly courageous. It is incredibly gratifying to him that he is essentially free and able to participate in the debate that he helped trigger, to see the reforms that are underway, and to realize the amount of support he has around the world, where he really is considered to be a hero by hundreds of millions of people. He is very fulfilled and happy. I don't think he knows exactly what his future holds, but he knew what the consequences would be when he made the choice to bring all of this to public light.

RUDYARD GRIFFITHS: And you are adamant that he is not an instrument of an agenda of other intelligence agencies?

GLENN GREENWALD: He is somebody who risked his entire life to bring an end to mass surveillance. The idea that he would be operating on behalf of some foreign government to increase their own surveillance capabilities is absurd, and the people who make that accusation make it without a shred of evidence. It is something that ought not to be taken seriously.

RUDYARD GRIFFITHS: Glenn, we really look forward to the debate and we're going to be showing the debate on your terrific new web site, theintercept.com. It's going to be a fabulous conversation, and we're glad to have you here in Toronto.

GLENN GREENWALD: I'm looking forward to it. Thank you very much.

ALEXIS OHANIAN IN CONVERSATION
WITH RUDYARD GRIFFITHS

RUDYARD GRIFFITHS: We're back now with Alexis Ohanian. He is an accomplished guy, but you might know him best as the co-founder of the phenomenal social media site reddit. More importantly he's joining Glenn Greenwald tonight to argue against the motion, "Be it resolved: state surveillance is a legitimate defence of our freedoms."

Alexis, it's important to have you in this debate because in addition to being a relentless campaigner for a free and open Web, you are a guy who has some real tech savvy.

ALEXIS OHANIAN: Indeed.

RUDYARD GRIFFITHS: And some business chops.

ALEXIS OHANIAN: I'm the only tech nerd and businessperson in the debate tonight.

RUDYARD GRIFFITHS: Given your online entrepreneurial experience, I want to talk to you a little bit about your criticism of the current surveillance regime and how you think it impacts American companies that are trying to build Internet businesses that you might want to see grow the world over.

ALEXIS OHANIAN: It has a huge impact. I'm an investor in more than a hundred companies, thanks to the success I've had, so I see the effects of this every day. Countries like the United States and Canada have been attractive for businesses in part because we have a reputation for protecting an individual's right to privacy. We have benefited so much from tech innovation as a nation, and part of the reason for that was because people trusted what was on our servers. But it is no longer the case. The cost of enforcing privacy and safety, which we need to do, is estimated in the billions.

I'm very fond of saying the world is not flat but the World Wide Web is. And what that means is that the competitive edge that we have is not at all permanent; it means that the next Facebook or Google could just as easily come out of Berlin or Seoul from a technological standpoint. And there is a very good chance that will be more likely to happen simply because of the effects of mass surveillance.

RUDYARD GRIFFITHS: You are our token debater who is under forty tonight, so you are a lot closer in age to a lot of the people that have been closely following this whole issue of state surveillance. I think it has really galvanized the younger generation. Why do you think that is? How does the threat of state surveillance change the way your demographic, people your age and younger, think about the Web?

ALEXIS OHANIAN: The Internet provides us with so many advantages that we take for granted. Privacy allows us to experiment and to tinker; you could start the next Google from your laptop or experiment with a cool art project. The Internet is a source of innovation. The right to privacy, enshrined in the Fourth Amendment of the American Constitution, lets us know that we have the right to create without worrying that in every moment, in every second, someone is watching.

The same technology that has allowed so many of us to create amazing things that have changed our lives and changed the world is now enabling a level of mass surveillance that is just absolutely unacceptable. And I think my generation understands that particularly well because we have grown up with the Internet. We are very acutely aware of the implications of a program that slurps up everything within reach. My argument is that from a technologist's standpoint, what we are doing with mass surveillance in the name of security is actually making us less secure, and that in itself is a fundamental problem.

RUDYARD GRIFFITHS: Can you unpack that for us? Why do you think it is making us less secure?

ALEXIS OHANIAN: I don't want to nerd out too much, but one way of explaining it is that a lot of what we see the NSA doing in the name of security is sort of akin to law enforcement deducing that there is a special kind of key that can unlock every door in a town. And instead of notifying everyone and improving the system, they are holding it secret. They are betting on the fact that, hopefully, no one else breaks into every home and takes advantage of it, because they want to use that key to take advantage of some bad person someday.

But the reality is, we are not just talking about a town, we are talking about the World Wide Web. Because what is stopping a Chinese hacker from doing the same thing? Who is stopping some other nefarious actor from acting on these vulnerabilities? Those are the kinds of concerns I have. It is wholly untenable.

RUDYARD GRIFFITHS: How would you respond to the older generation who might say your generation doesn't really know what it is like to face an actual existential threat, like the Second World War or the Cold War? So what would you say to critics who say: "Get over your privacy. Grow up and understand that the world is a dangerous place, and there are dangerous people out there who are trying to hurt us, and we need these tools to help us find the bad guys?"

ALEXIS OHANIAN: I agree: it is a dangerous world. But we need to make sure we use this new technology in the smartest way possible. It is not really a choice between some amount of privacy and some amount of security. It really comes down to using the technology for the best means to ensure security without violations of privacy. The issue is bigger than just the threats to our national security, the sort of terrorist bogeymen that we hear about. Online security is fundamental to America's success because it sets the stage for economic strength and economic security, which is part of national security.

RUDYARD GRIFFITHS: What do you think is the future of this debate? Do you think there is the potential that places like Canada, the United States, and Europe will want to put more controls on intelligence agencies and de-escalate? Or do you think it is really tough for politicians to say: "I'd love to deal with your privacy concerns now, but I know you will kick me out of office tomorrow if there is another 9/11 and it wasn't caught on my watch." Are you sympathetic to that political kind of conundrum?

ALEXIS OHANIAN: These politicians have a duty to us. We employ them, we fund their salaries, and we fire them when we need to. I think what they must hear now is that an overwhelming number of us in the West are not willing to make these security trade-offs. Many decision-makers have taken a heavy-handed approach to surveillance and much of it has been done largely in secret.

We've had some of the highest-ranking officials in American intelligence departments lying under oath to Congress about what they were doing. Who is watching the watchers? We've had our trust betrayed, and now the onus is on our elected officials to win back that trust through transparency.

RUDYARD GRIFFITHS: Edward Snowden: traitor or patriot?

ALEXIS OHANIAN: Patriot.

RUDYARD GRIFFITHS: The answer for you is obvious but explain why you think he deserves accolades? I assume you would support him returning to the United States tomorrow as a free citizen without charge?

ALEXIS OHANIAN: I've gone on the record a lot in various news outlets about this matter. The men behind the Pentagon Papers and Mr. Daniel Ellsberg have spoken out as voices of sympathy for Edward. They were also whistle-blowers who were able to bring some transparency to a really dark period of American history. Edward has endured quite a lot in the name of what I genuinely think is a really incredible, heroic act of patriotism. This is an opportunity for all of us as Americans, as Canadians, as believers in free societies, to look inward and say what kind of countries do we want to be? Do we want to be countries that live up to the ideals of our founding fathers and the founding documents that support civil liberties?

I was in college when 9/11 happened. Over a decade has passed, and I feel like we have an opportunity now to take an honest and hopefully patient and, frankly, critical look at laws that were passed and actions that have been taken since then. I know that these were undertaken with the best of intentions, but I think they require some re-evaluation.

RUDYARD GRIFFITHS: We're going to stop here but the big debate happens tonight. Again, terrific to have you here in Toronto.

ALEXIS OHANIAN: Thank you for having me. A real pleasure.

ALAN DERSHOWITZ IN CONVERSATION
WITH RUDYARD GRIFFITHS

RUDYARD GRIFFITHS: Welcome back to our interviews with our debaters tonight. I'm joined by storied lawyer, renowned Harvard academic, and celebrated civil libertarian Alan Dershowitz. He is joining Michael Hayden to argue in favour of our resolution, "Be it resolved: state surveillance is a legitimate defence of our freedoms." Professor Dershowitz, a real pleasure to have you here in Toronto. Thank you for coming to this debate.

ALAN DERSHOWITZ: Thank you.

RUDYARD GRIFFITHS: Let's start with a question that is probably on the minds of a lot of people. You are celebrated as one of America's foremost civil libertarians, yet you are joining Michael Hayden to argue for some measure of state surveillance. Can you explain what led you to this viewpoint?

ALAN DERSHOWITZ: I believe that state surveillance, reasonably controlled and constrained, helps promote liberty and helps to protect against terrorism. For me, one of the greatest threats to our liberties would be another 9/11, and I want to do everything reasonable to avoid it. Surveillance helped us win the Second World War because we were able to break the Japanese and German codes. Would anybody say we shouldn't have done that? I think even my distinguished opponents will acknowledge that some surveillance is necessary. The question is, how do we create a system which permits the kind of creative intelligence necessary to pre-empt another 9/11 without intruding too deeply on the privacy rights of individuals?

RUDYARD GRIFFITHS: Since the Snowden leaks almost a year ago, do you feel this debate has gone too far in terms of people advancing what they think of as privacy under threat? I think, for example, that Glenn Greenwald and Alexis Ohanian would say that privacy is in dire threat today in the United States. Would you agree?

ALAN DERSHOWITZ: Americans, unlike Canadians, tend to overreact to everything and tend to speak in extreme terms — we have to avoid that. About ten years ago I wrote a book called *Rights from Wrongs* in which I demonstrate that rights come out of the perception of wrongs. We've seen wrongs in the case of surveillance. There is no question the NSA revelations disclose many wrongs. But rights will grow out of that. The question is: Will we create a balance or will we allow the pendulum to swing too far against security and too much in favour of privacy?

'RUDYARD GRIFFITHS: What do you think might make the pendulum swing too far in the favour of privacy? What is being lost in that trade?

ALAN DERSHOWITZ: We lose our ability to pre-empt terrorist attacks and to use our technological advantage against terrorism. I don't want to give up our technological advantage. My fear is if we had another 9/11, we could see even greater setbacks in civil liberties and human rights.

RUDYARD GRIFFITHS: Part of this debate focuses on what happens within liberal democracies. I think everybody seems a little less concerned about the spying that is going on against non-citizens outside of the country. If you look at the NSA programs within the United States specifically, this idea of bulk collection has been presented as a paramount threat to security by some, including Glenn Greenwald. Do you think this is an exaggeration?

ALAN DERSHOWITZ: I haven't seen any diminution of First Amendment rights. We have full ability to be critical of our government — nobody should be fearful of what we say in public. But we have to make sure that we don't allow too much government surveillance and that we have constraints and controls over what they do. Mass collection is a very serious concern but it didn't start with modern technology. We used to have mail watches where the government, without a warrant, could look at the envelopes of every piece of mail that was sent through the postal authorities. We have long had searches of phone logs — the metadata has always been subject to searches without warrants. Now with modern technology there is simply so much more metadata; you can virtually track someone's movements by just looking at the metadata involving emails. So we need to have new rules that constrain this surveillance.

RUDYARD GRIFFITHS: But would you say the abolition of the practice itself is going too far?

ALAN DERSHOWITZ: Absolutely. I don't think we should be throwing out babies with the bathwater. We should not be losing our technological advantage because there have been abuses. This is a work-in-progress, and we have to make sure that what we come to in the end is a balance between privacy and security.

RUDYARD GRIFFITHS: Let's talk about Edward Snowden. We were just speaking with Alexis minutes ago, and he says Snowden is a great American hero and should be welcomed back into the United States with a ticker tape parade and given the full advantages he had before his remarkable leaks. What do you think?

ALAN DERSHOWITZ: I think it's a great idea. He should be welcomed back with a parade and then be arrested and put on trial and have to defend himself in court the way that Martin Luther King Jr. did. Snowden can claim that he was a civil disobedient and let a jury decide. That is the way we do it in America. The very fact that he disclosed that we are listening to Chancellor [Angela] Merkel's conversations shows that he doesn't care about the Fourth Amendment or American constitutional rights. Snowden stole material and exposed surveillance that we do very properly, but he also disclosed abuses and for that we ought to be thankful. When you engage in civil disobedience you ought to accept the consequences and not run away to another country.

RUDYARD GRIFFITHS: If you were sitting on that hypothetical jury, how would you decide?

ALAN DERSHOWITZ: I'd have to hear the evidence first and I might very well decide to acquit. But I would hold him in greater respect if he were willing to subject himself to the American legal system.

RUDYARD GRIFFITHS: How do you feel about the fact that he has sought and received shelter in Russia, which at this very moment is increasingly in opposition to the United

States due to a declining situation in the Ukraine and other geopolitical hot spots?

ALAN DERSHOWITZ: Russia will probably be increasingly in opposition not only to the United States but to all Western democracies that care deeply about the rule of law. I don't blame him for trying to seek asylum wherever he could get it. He was also trying to seek asylum in some South American countries. But he should do what Martin Luther King Jr. and Gandhi did, which is face the consequences of his civil disobedience and pay the price for breaking the law. When you are a true civil disobedient, you don't run away.

RUDYARD GRIFFITHS: Where do you think this debate is headed? Right now your own president has announced a series of reforms to surveillance he would like to see, including some additional congressional oversight. Do you think that is enough to allay a reasonable person's concerns about these programs as they stand?

ALAN DERSHOWITZ: Nobody knows because we don't know what is out there. We don't know what the NSA and the CIA and other organizations — whose existences we might not even be aware of — are doing. And it is hard to have a full debate in the absence of knowledge. We definitely need more disclosure and revelation so that we can have a full debate to decide how to strike the appropriate balance. One thing we have to do is dramatically change the nature of the FISA Court — the court that hands out warrants as if they were Christmas presents. We need to have real courts with advocates on both sides, assessing every single case and balancing the need for security versus the need for privacy, which we don't have right now.

RUDYARD GRIFFITHS: It seems that the very disclosure of surveillance is undermining the United States' capabilities and potentially weakening American security?

ALAN DERSHOWITZ: That's exactly right.

RUDYARD GRIFFITHS: So how do we have this debate if we have incomplete information?

ALAN DERSHOWITZ: That's what makes the debate so much more difficult than usual, but we can learn more than we know now. Snowden could have revealed the program without revealing the contents of the documents in question, or the contents of the program itself. That would have been a partial act of civil disobedience. Or he could have revealed the contents of improperly obtained material against American citizens without revealing the facts or the content of properly revealed information against foreigners or foreign leaders. We need more nuance and more balance in terms of how to conduct the debate.

RUDYARD GRIFFITHS: Well we hope we are going to have more knowledge after tonight's debate. Alan Dershowitz, thank you so much for coming to Toronto to be part of this conversation.

ALAN DERSHOWITZ: I'm looking forward to it. Thank you.

MICHAEL HAYDEN IN CONVERSATION
WITH RUDYARD GRIFFITHS

RUDYARD GRIFFITHS: This is our last in a series of four interviews we're conducting before the debate tonight. We welcome General Michael Hayden, a distinguished military officer who has served in a number of high-level posts in the United States such as head of the NSA and the head of the CIA. General Hayden, thank you so much for coming to Toronto to be a part of this debate.

MICHAEL HAYDEN: My pleasure. Thank you.

RUDYARD GRIFFITHS: General Hayden, there are many different arguments to be made for and against the current system of state surveillance in both the United States and the wider world. What is the key point you hope this audience leaves with from your side of the debate?

MICHAEL HAYDEN: This is not a discussion between the forces of good and evil, or between the forces of light and darkness. My country's founding document said that we're doing this independence thing for three reasons: life, liberty, and the pursuit of happiness. Now, sometimes those three things get a bit competitive. The democratic government and the people have to make decisions about how much emphasis to place on each. For example, how much emphasis do we put on the value of life, which translates to security and safety, as opposed to liberty, which translates to issues of privacy and transparency? Those things fluctuate, and so we need an honest discussion as a society, and we have to make tough choices. In essence, what I want to suggest to people is that it's complicated.

RUDYARD GRIFFITHS: Next month will be the anniversary of Snowden's leak. What fact do you think has been either obscured or ignored in this debate?

MICHAEL HAYDEN: What a great year. An awful lot of the data out there has been misunderstood. Part of that is simply that this information is hard to understand, so things get put out there without explanation. For example, the media had a heat map that showed how many millions of metadata events were taken from France, Spain, and Norway, and immediately the stories became, "we're ripping off 60 or 70 million metadata events per month from those countries in Europe."

The reality was that those countries were giving us

metadata that had very often been collected elsewhere, like in Afghanistan. This data is complicated and has often been misrepresented. My second point is that there are people out there who want to tell the surveillance story in the darkest way possible and who want to take the narrative into the gloomiest corner of the room.

My government, and my old agencies, have been flat-footed in responding to the story. There is a natural tendency in the intelligence and security fields to not want to engage publicly. Surveillance best succeeds in secret; however, much of it is no longer confidential. The people who are the keepers of the facts need to take part in the debate to ensure everyone has as much information as possible.

I believe criticism of the bulk collection program is okay once you've taken the time to understand how carefully it is run and how useful it has been. You have to work your way through all of those hoops before legitimately being able to complain about it.

RUDYARD GRIFFITHS: Glenn Greenwald represents the views of a lot of people who say, "I'm all for bugging Osama bin Laden's cellphone but just don't collect my data." Can the NSA succeed at its mission by just siloing out the supposed or alleged terrorists or threats and leaving all the rest of us out of it?

MICHAEL HAYDEN: Sure, why not? Most of us are not very interesting. Most of us, in fact, are boring. The NSA, CSEC here in Canada, and the GCHQ in Great Britain don't have a prurient interest to look into people's lives. I'd love to just listen to bin Laden's phone, but how do I know which particular phone is his? How do I arrive at that reality? Well, I have to swim in the data stream. I have to go out on a bit of a journey of discovery, and once I find out which one is his, rest assured, you're a waste of time.

Here's the main issue: most people in the big, Western democracies are accustomed to their intelligence agencies going after the Soviet Union. And trust me, I love that enemy — they were slow moving, oligarchic, and a technologically inferior nation. I miss those guys.

No one argued or complained when we were intercepting a Soviet microwave signal out of strategic rocket forces headquarters in Moscow, or hopping up over the Ural Mountains to intercontinental ballistic missile fields in the Far East, looking for words of interest like *launch*. That doesn't exist anymore. The twenty-first century equivalent of that dangerous signal are *proliferator*, *terrorist*, *narco-trafficker*, *money laundering*, and emails coexisting with your emails and mine on the same integrated telecommunications grid. This really isn't an expansion of surveillance; it is actually your surveillance agencies modernizing to intercept twenty-first century technology.

But surveillance agencies have become aggressive in the twenty-first century; they have worked within the law but right up to the edges of it. The reality is these agencies can't undertake a modern mission without looking at everyone's stuff. We need to find a way for citizens of Canada, the United States, Great Britain, Australia, and New Zealand to have trust and faith in their security services to go after the bad guys, bump into your stuff, and be good enough to grab only the bad guys' information and honest enough not to touch yours. I said almost that exact sentence to the House of Representatives of the United States in open session, eighteen months before 9/11.

RUDYARD GRIFFITHS: You've said elsewhere that the NSA was drowning in a wave of data when you took it over in the late 1990s.

MICHAEL HAYDEN: Yes.

RUDYARD GRIFFITHS: And that these programs evolved over time to not only respond to that data but to see that data as an opportunity to become more efficient and more effective. Looking back on your own career and the Snowden revelations, do you feel that you made the right decision or was there a mistake made along the way? Did it go too far? Was there another path that we could have taken?

MICHAEL HAYDEN: There isn't another technological path that I think we could have taken. But even President Obama's commission looked at this bulk collection–metadata approach, which is the way you find the needle in the haystack, and they strongly recommend that the NSA and the United States find technological ways to discover communications of interest without having to do bulk collection and that kind of analysis. I told them it was a great idea, but no one had any idea how to do it. I actually wrote on the margins of that report when I was reading it, "We'll clap our hands and sprinkle fairy dust until that happens." So until we develop new technology, the best tool we have to deal with volume is to embrace it. We can't be defeated by the fact that the haystack is getting bigger and bigger and bigger, but instead we need to turn around and accept it. We need to use the location, the number, and the pattern of the haystacks themselves to keep you safe.

RUDYARD GRIFFITHS: Where do you think this whole field is going? The cost of processing data continues to collapse, and computing power continues to grow. You're right that Canada and the United States afford privacy and other constitutional protections, but the Chinese and the Russians don't care about your privacy rights or mine. Surely their capacities are growing to collect our metadata, to scoop our emails and phone conversations and all that stuff. Are we in an arms race that leads to the end of privacy as we know it?

MICHAEL HAYDEN: You don't need government surveillance agencies to threaten privacy as we know it.

RUDYARD GRIFFITHS: Do you mean the corporate sector?

MICHAEL HAYDEN: Yes, exactly. We talk about the NSA having metadata. But actually, the NSA doesn't data mine the metadata. The NSA just contacts someone when it has got a bad number, a seed number, and tries to attach a contact chain from it. The private sector does that all the time. It packages you up and sells you and your info to other people who want to sell you things.

RUDYARD GRIFFITHS: It sounds pretty egregious when you explain it that way; they're doing it for profit.

MICHAEL HAYDEN: Right, and people complain when I do it to keep them safe!

RUDYARD GRIFFITHS: Can you explain to me why people are giving the corporations a pass but seem to be beating the you-know-what out of government for it?

MICHAEL HAYDEN: Two reasons. First is habit. We in the Western world are accustomed to having our privacy threatened by government. And frankly the instinct to distrust government may not be an appropriate response to the modern world. The other reason is more concrete: the government can put you in jail, but Google, Microsoft, and Yahoo can't. So there is also a real emphasis on having a more limited government than the private sector.

RUDYARD GRIFFITHS: I've asked all the other debaters about Edward Snowden. Do you think he betrayed his country? Or is he, as some have said, an American hero who should be brought back to the country of his birth and afforded every right and privilege for what he has done?

MICHAEL HAYDEN: I'll combine the two options. He's not an American hero — he did betray his country — but I'd be delighted for him to come back to the United States.

RUDYARD GRIFFITHS: And what would you want to happen to him?

MICHAEL HAYDEN: I'd like to see a jury of his peers decide. He claims he performed a heroic action. He claims he couldn't follow the path of a true whistle-blower, because as a contractor he didn't have the same kinds of legal protections. He chose a course of action that has him in exile in one of the most autocratic states on the planet. How much worse could it have been if he had decided to just take a flight to Washington rather than to Hong Kong and met with Senator Wyden, Senator Udall, or Senator Feinstein instead of the group from WikiLeaks?

For the record, most of what has been revealed from the Snowden cache of documents has absolutely nothing to do with American, Canadian, British, or Australian privacy matters, but it has everything to do with how those countries are legally collecting legitimate foreign intelligence.

RUDYARD GRIFFITHS: We are going to find out more about this tonight. Michael Hayden, thank you for coming to Toronto.

MICHAEL HAYDEN: Thank you. It was my pleasure.

Post-Debate Commentary

POST-DEBATE COMMENTARY
BY RON DEIBERT

Ever since the first Edward Snowden leak hit the news on June 5, 2013, American citizens, government officials, and company executives have publicly debated its implications: Is the NSA violating the Fourth and Fifth Amendments of the U.S. Constitution? Do they have confidence in the existing system of oversight? What did telecommunications and Internet companies know (or not know) about PRISM and other programs like it before they were revealed? And how much should these companies disclose to their users about such programs?

During the Munk Debate on May 2, 2014, we all enjoyed a slice of what vigorous public debate is all about. The former head of the NSA, General Michael Hayden, argued that the leaked Snowden documents were being taken out of context and that citizens should trust that the NSA is doing a good job within well-defined limits. Renowned Harvard scholar Alan Dershowitz backed him up with well-reasoned philosophical arguments about the need to trade off some liberty in exchange for security, given the nature of today's distributed threats. reddit co-founder Alexis Ohanian took the industry view, explaining how the NSA's subversion of the Internet for mass surveillance is hurting innovation and the bottom line. Journalist Glenn Greenwald, the night's main attraction, argued the NSA could not be trusted, that its "collect it all" mentality and history of deceit make it dangerously out of control. He had the evening's best zinger: How can we trust the NSA when it says it carefully restricts what analysts can do with all of the data it collects when it couldn't even prevent a system administrator like Edward Snowden from scooping up millions of documents from right under its nose?

Missing from the debate was the elephant in the room. The room being Roy Thomson Hall, located in downtown Toronto, Canada, and that elephant being Canada's own system of state surveillance. Although the name of our own NSA, the Communications Security Establishment of Canada (CSEC), was briefly referenced once or twice, the details of its operations were left unexamined by the debaters, which is a shame, for the Canadian situation offers a remarkable contrast to the one that exists in the United States.

Whereas the NSA's operations are overseen by three branches of government, including being subject to regular congressional oversight committees and the scrutiny of eleven judges of the FISA Court, Canada's CSEC does not report to Parliament, is answerable only to the minister of defence, and is overseen by a single retired judge who issues an annual "review." In the United States, the NSA revelations have brought about widespread calls for reforms and prompted President Obama to set up the President's Review Group on surveillance. This review group made over forty recommendations on everything from civil liberties to the FISA Court itself, some of which were referenced explicitly by President Obama in a major public address to the nation. Here in Canada, by contrast, government officials have hardly acknowledged the revelations at all, have not proposed any reforms, and have responded to CSEC revelations with statements that simply reiterate official boilerplate policy.

Big American Internet and telecommunications companies, as well as social media giants, have begun issuing detailed transparency reports about government requests for user data, with some going so far as to take the government to court to reinforce their right to notify users when such requests are made. In contrast, the Canadian telecommunications industry has stuck to what can only be described as a shameful silence — even in the face of alarming statistics that suggest companies routinely hand over user data to government agencies millions of times a year without a warrant.

The Munk debaters missed a major opportunity to bring up Canada. In spite of their differences, it was clear that everyone on the stage believed that there are real threats that need to be dealt with, and that liberal democratic governments should deal with them under some system of oversight and accountability. The Canadian case could have served as a great example of the type of flawed system that everyone could agree should be avoided at all costs — a retrograde model from the Cold War era unsuited to the challenges of twenty-first century liberal democracy.

Then again, maybe it was appropriate that Canada was not brought up during the debate. A poll undertaken by the Canadian Journalists for Free Expression, whose results were released just prior to the debate, showed that at least 60 percent of Canadians do not seem concerned that the government is monitoring their communications. If Canadians don't care about the issue in the first place, why should we expect our American visitors to bring it up?

It is common for Canadians to feel superior to Americans when it comes to public discourse, to point to the trash-talking and polarizing cable news networks we eavesdrop on from north of the border. But the Munk Debates reminded us we have a lot to learn from our American cousins when it comes to maturely discussing an issue so fundamental to society as the appropriate balance to strike between security and privacy in a liberal democracy. Never mind debates, we have barely acknowledged the subject in civil discourse.

Ron Deibert is director of the Citizen Lab and the Canada Centre for Global Security Studies at the Munk School of Global Affairs, University of Toronto, and the author of Black Code: Surveillance, Privacy, and the Dark Side of the Internet.

POST-DEBATE COMMENTARY BY ANN CAVOUKIAN

As Glenn Greenwald so eloquently put it, "nobody opposes targeted surveillance." There is no question that some targeted surveillance is needed and, at times, vitally necessary. But, like Mr. Greenwald and Mr. Ohanian, I cannot accept the zero-sum views of massive state surveillance expounded by General Hayden and Mr. Dershowitz that effectively sacrifice privacy in the name of security. This false trade-off is invariably destructive in free and open societies. It is not only ineffective, it is also unnecessary and completely without justification.

Both Mr. Dershowitz and General Hayden's viewpoints appear to be based not on fact but on dogma. In the debate, both implied it was a fact that the NSA's tactics had prevented terrorism attacks on numerous occasions. Since 9/11, the NSA has been collecting an incalculable amount of data on everyone. After repeatedly exaggerating the alleged security payoff, another former head of the NSA, General Keith Alexander, finally acknowledged that "only one, or perhaps two" minor plots had been discovered as a direct result of the NSA's programs. How can such tenuous claims justify invading the privacy and liberty of millions of people? The simple answer is that they cannot. Two presidential review boards have examined the NSA's mass telephone metadata surveillance programs and reached the same conclusions: (1) these programs were not effective in catching terrorists, (2) there were significant harms associated with innocent people being incorrectly marked as terrorist threats (false positives), and (3) the bulk collection of data should be stopped — now. While progress may be slow in bringing about much-needed changes to these programs, I applaud our neighbours to the south for publicly addressing these issues.

As we clearly witnessed in the debate, many points of view on this issue must be aired publicly, including here in Canada. Yet there has been a total wall of silence from the federal government and Communications Security Establishment Canada (CSEC) — we know disturbingly little about how this agency conducts its mass metadata surveillance programs. Our government has yet to answer pivotal questions about privacy and security. Meanwhile, not only is it becoming increasingly clear that CSEC works very closely with the NSA, but we now know that we are apparently the "envy" of the NSA (which believes a surveillance state is necessary)!

General Hayden was quoted in the *Globe and Mail* as praising the "agility" of CSEC and its "ability to push through secret surveillance programs without generating any pushback from politicians or judges." As a Canadian, I find this not only extremely troubling but also deeply embarrassing.

At the bottom of this so-called agility in Canada is a lack of privacy protection, transparency requirements, and accountability measures. Indeed, CSEC operations rely on ministerial approval with secret privacy protections and little, if any, transparency and accountability. To obtain authorization for any type of data collection or surveillance, CSEC goes straight to the minister of defence, with no judicial oversight whatsoever. CSEC's only form of public accountability rests on a single annual review undertaken by the CSEC commissioner and his small staff. This report is only submitted to Parliament after being reviewed by the minister of national defence. Meanwhile, year after year, the commissioner's reports have quietly alluded to inadequate and missing information, excessive delays in getting answers, and an inability to reach definitive conclusions about the lawfulness of CSEC's activities.

This kind of "trust me" model advanced by General Hayden, Mr. Dershowitz, and CSEC is wearing thin. The need for operational secrecy must not stand in the way of public accountability. Canadians deserve to have a legal framework that allows for necessary, warranted surveillance and provides for strong privacy protections, transparency, and oversight. In a free and open society, we must have both.

Ann Cavoukian was Ontario's Information and Privacy Commissioner from 1997 until her retirement in June 2014. One of the world's leading privacy experts, she is the key proponent of Privacy by Design.

ACKNOWLEDGEMENTS

The Munk Debates are the product of the public-spiritedness of a remarkable group of civic-minded organizations and individuals. First and foremost, these debates would not be possible without the vision and leadership of the Aurea Foundation. Founded in 2006 by Peter and Melanie Munk, the Aurea Foundation supports Canadian individuals and institutions involved in the study and development of public policy. The debates are the foundation's signature initiative, a model for the kind of substantive public policy conversation Canadians can foster globally. Since the creation of the debates in 2008, the foundation has underwritten the entire cost of each semi-annual event. The debates have also benefited from the input and advice of members of the board of the foundation, including Mark Cameron, Andrew Coyne, Devon Cross, Allan Gotlieb, George Jonas, Margaret MacMillan, Anthony Munk, Robert Prichard and Janice Stein.

For her contribution to the preliminary edit of the book, the debate organizers would like to thank Jane McWhinney.

Since their inception the Munk Debates have sought to take the discussions that happen at each event to national and international audiences. Here the debates have benefited immeasurably from a partnership with Canada's national newspaper, the *Globe and Mail*, and the counsel of its editor-in-chief, David Walmsley.

With the publication of this superb book, House of Anansi Press is helping the debates reach new audiences in Canada and around the world. The debates' organizers would like to thank Anansi chair Scott Griffin and president and publisher Sarah MacLachlan for their enthusiasm for this book project and insights into how to translate the spoken debate into a powerful written intellectual exchange.

ABOUT THE DEBATERS

MICHAEL HAYDEN is a retired four-star general who served as director of the CIA, director of the National Security Agency (NSA), and chief of the Central Security Service (CSS). General Hayden has also served as the principal deputy director of national intelligence, the highest-ranking military intelligence officer in America. He is currently a principal at the Chertoff Group, a security consultancy co-founded by Homeland Security Secretary Michael Chertoff, and a distinguished visiting professor at the George Mason University School of Public Policy.

ALAN DERSHOWITZ is considered one of America's pre-eminent civil liberties lawyers. Until his retirement in December 2013, Dershowitz was the Felix Frankfurter Professor of Law at Harvard Law School. He has published over one thousand articles in magazines, newspapers, journals, and blogs, including the *New York Times Magazine*, the *Washington Post*, and the *Wall Street Journal*, and is the author of thirty fiction and non-fiction books, including *Chutzpah*, the *New York Times* #1 bestseller. His books have been translated into many languages and have sold more than a million copies worldwide.

GLENN GREENWALD is a Pulitzer Prize–winning investigative journalist and columnist for First Look Media. Formerly a constitutional and civil lawyer, he is the author of three *New York Times*–bestselling books, including *How Would a Patriot Act?* and *With Liberty and Justice for Some*. In June 2013, Greenwald published the first of many stories related to classified NSA surveillance programs from the troves of documents leaked by Edward Snowden. His book on the subject, *No Place to Hide: Edward Snowden, the NSA, and the U.S. Surveillance State*, was released in April 2014.

ALEXIS OHANIAN is a serial Internet entrepreneur and co-founder of reddit, the social news web site used by over 100 million people each month. Named to the *Forbes* "30 Under 30: Technology" list two years in a row, he has been lauded as the "Mayor of the Internet" for rallying public opposition to the U.S. Congress's Stop Online Piracy Act. He is also the author of the national bestseller *Without Their Permission: How the 21st Century Will Be Made, Not Managed*.

ABOUT THE EDITOR

RUDYARD GRIFFITHS is Chair of the Munk Debates and President of the Peter and Melanie Munk Charitable Foundation. In 2006 he was named one of Canada's "Top 40 under 40" by the *Globe and Mail.* He is the editor of thirteen books on history, politics, and international affairs, including *Who We Are: A Citizen's Manifesto*, which was a *Globe and Mail* Best Book of 2009 and a finalist for the Shaughnessy Cohen Prize for Political Writing. He lives in Toronto with his wife and two children.

ABOUT THE MUNK DEBATES

The Munk Debates are Canada's premier public policy event. Held semi-annually, the debates provide leading thinkers with a global forum to discuss the major public policy issues facing the world and Canada. Each event takes place in Toronto in front of a live audience, and the proceedings are covered by domestic and international media. Participants in recent Munk Debates include Robert Bell, Tony Blair, John Bolton, Ian Bremmer, Daniel Cohn-Bendit, Paul Collier, Howard Dean, Hernando de Soto, Maureen Dowd, Gareth Evans, Mia Farrow, Niall Ferguson, William Frist, David Gratzer, Rick Hillier, Christopher Hitchens, Richard Holbrooke, Josef Joffe, Henry Kissinger, Charles Krauthammer, Paul Krugman, Lord Nigel Lawson, Stephen Lewis, David Li, Bjørn Lomborg, Lord Peter Mandelson, Elizabeth May, George Monbiot, Caitlin Moran, Dambisa Moyo, Vali Nasr, Camille Paglia, Samantha Power, David Rosenberg,

Hanna Rosin, Lawrence Summers, Amos Yadlin, and Fareed Zakaria.

The Munk Debates are a project of the Aurea Foundation, a charitable organization established in 2006 by philanthropists Peter and Melanie Munk to promote public policy research and discussion. For more information, visit www.munkdebates.com.

ABOUT THE INTERVIEWS

Rudyard Griffiths interviews with Glenn Greenwald, Alexis Ohanian, Alan Dershowitz, and Michael Hayden were recorded on May 2, 2014. The Aurea Foundation is gratefully acknowledged for permission to reprint excerpts from the following:

(p. 57) "Glenn Greenwald in Conversation," by Rudyard Griffiths. Copyright © 2014 Aurea Foundation. Transcribed by Rondi Adamson.

(p. 67) "Alexis Ohanian in Conversation," by Rudyard Griffiths. Copyright © 2014 Aurea Foundation. Transcribed by Rondi Adamson.

(p. 75) "Alan Dershowitz in Conversation," by Rudyard Griffiths. Copyright © 2014 Aurea Foundation. Transcribed by Rondi Adamson.

(p. 83) "Michael Hayden in Conversation," by Rudyard Griffiths. Copyright © 2014 Aurea Foundation. Transcribed by Rondi Adamson.

ABOUT THE POST-DEBATE COMMENTARY

Ron Deibert's and Ann Cavoukian's post-debate commentaries were written on May 5, 2014. The Aurea Foundation wishes to thank Rudyard Griffiths for his assistance in commissioning these essays.

Are Men Obsolete?

Rosin and Dowd vs. Moran and Paglia

For the first time in history, will it be better to be a woman than a man in the upcoming century? Renowned author and editor Hanna Rosin and Pulitzer Prize–winning columnist Maureen Dowd challenge *New York Times*–bestselling author Caitlin Moran and trailblazing social critic Camille Paglia to debate the relative decline of the power and status of men in the workplace, the family, and society at large.

"Feminism was always wrong to pretend women could 'have it all.' It is not male society but Mother Nature who lays the heaviest burden on women."

— Camille Paglia

www.houseofanansi.com/munkdebates

Should We Tax the Rich More?

Krugman and Papandreou vs. Gingrich and Laffer

Is imposing higher taxes on the wealthy the best way for countries to reinvest in their social safety nets, education, and infrastructure while protecting the middle class? Or does raising taxes on society's wealth creators lead to capital flight, falling government revenues, and less money for the poor? Nobel Prize–winning economist Paul Krugman and former prime minister of Greece George Papandreou square off against former Speaker of the U.S. House of Representatives Newt Gingrich and famed economist Arthur Laffer to debate this key issue.

"The effort to finance big government through higher taxes is a direct assault on civil society."

— Newt Gingrich

Can the World Tolerate an Iran with Nuclear Weapons?

Krauthammer and Yadlin vs. Zakaria and Nasr

Is the case for a pre-emptive strike on Iran ironclad? Or can a nuclear Iran be a stabilizing force in the Middle East? Former Israel Defense Forces head of military intelligence Amos Yadlin, Pulitzer Prize–winning political commentator Charles Krauthammer, CNN host Fareed Zakaria, and Iranian-born academic Vali Nasr debate the consequences of a nuclear-armed Iran.

"Deterring Iran is fundamentally different from deterring the Soviet Union. You could rely on the latter but not the former."
— Charles Krauthammer

North America's Lost Decade?

Krugman and Rosenberg vs. Summers and Bremmer

The future of the North American economy is more uncertain than ever. In this edition of the Munk Debates, Nobel Prize–winning economist Paul Krugman and chief economist and strategist at Gluskin Sheff + Associates David Rosenberg square off against former U.S. Treasury secretary Lawrence Summers and bestselling author Ian Bremmer to tackle the resolution: Be it resolved North America faces a Japan-style era of high unemployment and slow growth.

"It's now impossible to deny the obvious, which is that we are not now, and have never been, on the road to recovery."

— Paul Krugman

Does the 21st Century Belong to China?
Kissinger and Zakaria vs. Ferguson and Li

Is China's rise unstoppable? Former U.S. Secretary of State Henry Kissinger and CNN's Fareed Zakaria pair off against leading historian Niall Ferguson and world-renowned Chinese economist David Daokui Li to debate China's emergence as a global force, the key geopolitical issue of our time.

This edition of The Munk Debate on China is the first formal public debate Dr. Kissinger has participated in on China's future.

"I have enormous difficulty imagining a world dominated by China . . . I believe the concept that any one country will dominate the world is, in itself, a misunderstanding of the world in which we live now."

— Henry Kissinger

www.houseofanansi.com/munkdebates

Hitchens vs. Blair

Christopher Hitchens vs. Tony Blair

Intellectual juggernaut and staunch atheist Christopher Hitchens goes head-to-head with former British prime minister Tony Blair, one of the Western world's most openly devout political leaders, on the age-old question: Is religion a force for good in the world? Few world leaders have had a greater hand in shaping current events than Blair; few writers have been more outspoken and polarizing than Hitchens.

Sharp, provocative, and thoroughly engrossing, *Hitchens vs. Blair* is a rigorous and electrifying intellectual sparring match on the contentious questions that continue to dog the topic of religion in our globalized world.

"If religious instruction were not allowed until the child had attained the age of reason, we would be living in a very different world."

— Christopher Hitchens

www.houseofanansi.com/munkdebates

The Munk Debates: Volume One

Edited by Rudyard Griffiths; Introduction by Peter Munk

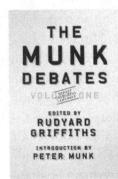

Launched in 2008 by philanthropists Peter and Melanie Munk, the Munk Debates is Canada's premier international debate series, a highly anticipated cultural event that brings together the world's brightest minds.

This volume includes the first five debates in the series, and features twenty leading thinkers and doers arguing for or against provocative resolutions that address pressing public policy concerns, such as the future of global security, the implications of humanitarian intervention, the effectiveness of foreign aid, the threat of climate change, and the state of health care in Canada and the United States.

"By trying to highlight the most important issues at crucial moments in the global conversation, these debates not only profile the ideas and solutions of some of our brightest thinkers and doers, but crystallize public passion and knowledge, helping to tackle some global challenges confronting humankind."

— Peter Munk

www.houseofanansi.com/munkdebates